# All You Can Be

## Empowering Awakening Angels

### Nicky Hamid, MA., Ph.D.

INFI∞ITY
PUBLISHING.COM

Copyright © 2009 by Nicky Hamid

ISBN 0-7414-5285-5

*Published by:*

**INFI∞ITY**
PUBLISHING.COM

*1094 New DeHaven Street, Suite 100*
*West Conshohocken, PA 19428-2713*
*Info@buybooksontheweb.com*
*www.buybooksontheweb.com*
*Toll-free (877) BUY BOOK*
*Local Phone (610) 941-9999*
*Fax (610) 941-9959*

*Printed in the United States of America*

*Published July 2010*

# CONTENTS

# Introduction

One of the premises on which this book is written is that there is no such thing as an accident. The unexplained and the unexpected is one of the essential characteristics of our experiencing life, and if we can accept that we do not have to know everything to live fully, then we allow for the unknown to be a part of how we will experience life. So the fact that you are reading this book is no accident. You have picked up a token of energy that is connected to all that the words are connected to, and those words stand for an expression of my knowing as the writer. There is something in this book for you, otherwise you would not have been drawn to it or picked it up in the first place.

So if you decide to read on then make some intent to be open to whatever it is that you need that the words, the ideas will trigger within you. My views, my ideas, my point of view is only that, my view. I do not claim that what is contained in my work represents any definitive or absolute Truth. I believe that each reader will have their own working truth and, therefore, I know that you will read and take unto yourself only that which resonates with you. However, be careful not to discard what you do resonate with if you read anything you cannot go along with. Just put those ideas aside to examine, or not, at a later date.

Furthermore, it is important not to accept what I say as true just because I say it. Be aware that if you find things that make sense to you and help you, the truths therein were really already yours. It was simply that you were just not consciously aware of them up till now.

This book is about waking up or remembering things that you have long forgotten, have dismissed, or have bypassed in your need to keep your footing in these chaotic times, and it is my greatest joy if what you read here can help you remember.

As you read do trust yourself, and if questions arise, trust that the answers will be given to you. Sincere seeking will always be satisfied if you stay open. Just as you have been led to this book for something it can spark in you, your quest for understanding will be met through many avenues, events and people. So enjoy the trip we will make together as you read, along with all the energy and knowing of those who have read this work before you.

You may also find that, in coming back to the book and allowing it to open at an unspecified page, it will provide you with answers or guidance in your life. If you believe and trust in the power of your intent then this procedure will bear its fruit.

# Chapter 1

# The Great Change

Now is the winter of our discontent,

Made glorious summer by this sun – Shakespeare

## Something Profound is Happening to Us All

It appears that something monumental is happening to all of humanity. Something has been stirring in you for a very long time and as we move further into the 21$^{st}$ century something radical, profound and often scary is happening to everyone. It is as though the very core of you has been shaken loose and there is a continual and persistent call within you that things are not right. The world is going mad and the ship is sinking. You are experiencing a deep discontent and though you can gain temporary relief in some activities nothing seems to last or satisfy this feeling of lack and being unfulfilled.

There is a deep yearning within you for a happiness which is more lasting and authentic. You are constantly being made aware that there is a deep gulf between the you that you want to be and the you that is living in the world at this time. You are aware, of a disturbing difference between the role you are playing with others in your life and the real self that you feel privately inside you. It is like being only half alive and sometimes like you are looking at life through a tunnel or a murky screen. You want to feel more alive and vital than you often feel nowadays. There is an unstoppable, painful pull to express the feelings that will release you from the prison of the world of your past and the past of humankind.

1

Somehow you know instinctively that the world that you are experiencing, particularly the world of people, is not the way it is supposed to be. Surely there is another way? Why don't others see it? Why is there so much hate and violence, pain and despair? There has to be another way. Where can I find it? How can I break free when there are so many things holding me back? How can my world change for the better when there is so much wrong with it? Being only one person I am powerless to make any real difference. Where would I start even if I could? These questions are very real and if they express your sentiments you are not alone.

Everything is in a state of change and everyone on this planet, at there own level of awareness and understanding, is feeling this pressure. The world we thought we knew is in a state of change and is being turned upside down. Some might call it upheaval for this is certainly how the changes are being experienced within you in your daily life. Nothing seems reliable or stable anymore. What appeared to have some form of reliability and consistency no longer appears to stay still. It is as if the world is wobbling, and you along with it.

Many of you have thought seriously about, or have activated, or have recently changed your job, where you live, a major relationship with another, or have had to have a major rethink from an illness, injury or death to a loved one or friend. These changes have required you to reassess where you are going and what you want in your life. Frequently, however, you will be left with the feeling that even though the changes in your life have been beneficial that they are not over and an unsettled feeling of "unfinished business" remains.

## Fear of the Inevitable Change

Doubt, uncertainty, and fear seem to be at the root of the disturbance within you. You know within the core of who you are, that you, and your life are changing and must change, and while you desire the transformation, you are afraid to let go of what you know. All the fears of your past are coming back to haunt you and no matter what you do they won't go away until you deal with them. Furthermore, the future seems so vague and uncertain as to appear blank and almost meaningless. Your hopes and dreams are so coloured by your past, and the present human view of powerlessness that is promulgated by the media and the conversations of people around you, that it is hard to see the future as filled with great promise and potential joy. Attempts on your part to direct your life towards a more positive outcome seem often swamped by the old patterns of negativity and victimhood.

So why is all this happening? What is causing this great discontent and feelings of confusion and disorientation that things are not working out? What is it that is causing the feelings of being out of balance and that either you are going mad or the world is mad and you wish you were not here?

## Our Planet is on the Move

If you are experiencing some, or all of these things, believe it or not, it can be a sign that something very positive is happening to you, and to the planet. These challenges and magnified feelings are, in most cases, a result of an extraordinary consciousness shift that Planet Earth and all kingdoms, including her human inhabitants, are undergoing. This shift has been called "The Shift of the Ages"... "The Great Consciousness Shift"... a "Quantum Evolutionary Leap"... "The Planetary Ascension"... "The Quickening"... "The Dawning of the Aquarian Age." The essence of the change is that we are shifting from our limited, material state of consciousness to a higher spiritual state of consciousness, free from many of the individual and collective problems of our present existence. We are evolving beyond the state in which fear, separation, struggle, and strife can thrive. We are growing into a more enlightened state that will be more characterized by love, unity, freedom, compassion, cooperation, and peace.

This shift is being enhanced by an increase of Transformational Light pouring into Earth's atmosphere. This light is the force behind cosmic evolution... the process of every created thing unfolding its full divine potential and moving up the ladder of consciousness (or frequency resonance). We are currently experiencing a long, sometimes rocky transition into this higher state. The whole of humanity is in a phase that may be likened to cosmic growing pains.

This transition began way back in the 1960s, and has been steadily escalating in intensity ever since. At first the Divine Light came in waves. Each time one of these waves of transformational light sweeps over the planet, Earth's vibration has raised to a slightly higher frequency, elevating the spirit of Earth - Gaia - along with us all, to a higher state of consciousness. The time in between waves has given us time to assimilate the new level of awareness and therefore has been hardly noticeable.

Now, the Divine Light has become more of a constant flow with an occasional ebb, rather than a series of waves. It is ever present in our atmosphere and the very atoms of ourselves, and is continually escalating. The effects are essentially the same, but even more intensified, and we are not getting much in the way of breaks to catch our breath. We are being forced to make a total shift in consciousness, in our way of seeing ourselves and our world.

## The Photon Belt

This Great Shift has been brought about by our entire solar system moving into a region of our galaxy whereby every place and space is being infused with light. This zone of intense and profound energy is referred to as the Photon Belt. During the procession of our Solar System around the

Great Central Sun of our galaxy, it must twice pass through a vast belt of creative radiation, the Photon Belt. During this cycle, which takes 25,860 years, there are two periods of darkness and two periods of light. There are two periods of 2000 years of total light, in which our entire planetary system will pass through the Photon Belt. The Photon Belt and its radiation are vehicles of transformation and transmutation of all matter and energy. It acts as a guardian barrier filtering out miscreated and denser energy of Earth and preventing it from escaping and contaminating higher levels of consciousness within our galaxy. Unless we are in accord with these energies, as we approach and enter the Photon Belt, we cannot hope to be a part of it and escape the negative influences of our creation and identification. In other words our consciousness has to align with the higher vibratory frequencies of the new environment that we are moving into. It will be impossible to remain on earth in our present physical form otherwise.

We entered the Photon Belt around the year 2000 which also marked our entrance into the fourth dimension as a people, planet, and consciousness. This means that all matter on our planet, including our bodies are being suffused with protons. You are literally being filled with light. It is destined that Earth be assured safe passage into and through the Photon Belt. It is our choice whether we also will make it through the transition. For many it will be a conscious choice to accept, accommodate, and act out the incoming Light consciousness. It will be a matter of learning to consciously allow the energy changes in our body, mind and emotions to work and to consciously develop a new way of seeing that will enable the incoming light to be active in our life. Above all our choice of love and freedom, and refusal to be governed by our fears, or accept the fears of the old ways, will provide the foundation for the unstoppable emergence of the new energies and consciousness.

We are emerging from our oppressive cocoon of darkness and, like the butterfly, can emerge as something extremely beautiful. That cocoon of darkness, despite its oppressiveness and negativity, has been our teacher. We are being offered the opportunity to break the fetters of this world of illusion, to turn the mirror around, and in its place perceive our true reality and the fact that we are Divine Beings going Home. In order to go home we must first experience a tremendous transformational process which will enable us to eliminate our negativity, awaken and remember who we really are and where we have been, and assume our bodies of light with full consciousness. This, in turn, will catapult us free of the enslaving energies of the third dimension into the fourth and fifth dimensions of the Photon Belt.

You are a vital part of the tremendous changes that are happening and the choice is clear. Why not make the conscious decision to take your path to become fully enlightened thereby beginning to welcome the changes that are occurring within and without? Why not make it your practice to make a conscious and daily commitment to this decision to take a broader and higher perspective in viewing yourself and your world? Why not gradually, steadily and stealthily, drop all the fears that make you feel a victim and take hold of the truth of your amazing Divinity? Change your perspective and you will change your world and your experience of it.

## Some Symptoms of the Energy Changes

Let us return for a moment to the nature of the pressures you will be facing at present. What are some of the major signs of this Great Shift that people are commonly experiencing?

1. We have already mentioned **the deep longing for something profoundly satisfying, a place that you somehow know is real and possible, a place that is Home.** This desire for your place of centre, of belonging, of peace and love and utter

connectedness will not go away and sometimes it is felt as a pleading, "Please just stop all this nonsense and let me go home". Yet it is not a desperate 'suicidal' feeling but rather yearning for your journey to be over and for you to be quietly and safely in your own home.

2. With everything from the past gradually coming to the surface to be cleared there is a **feeling of deep inner sadness for no apparent reason**. There is the sadness of leaving the past behind as you shed all the emotional and mental attachments to memories. There is also the deep anguish of the emotional pain of humanity you have experienced in your body. As it is naturally brought to the surface you will feel the great sadness especially for yourself.

3. Sometimes you may spontaneously **cry for no apparent reason,** or the slightest trigger, for example, from an item or scene on TV will set you off. On occasions these tears can become a deep sobbing. The flow of tears helps to release the past blocked and submerged energy within. There is much past pain to release and as we shall see it is a bridge to our understanding and compassion.

4. You may be prone to **sudden outbursts of frustration and anger** which may have been uncharacteristic of you in the past and that often seem out of proportion to the event that triggered it. These seem to express the feelings of refusal to be controlled or manipulated by another, or a breaking out of your own truth feelings. Given that even as children we have all had our truth trodden on, these feelings of anger are perfectly understandable and are part of our awakening and growing up.

5.  The inpouring of new frequencies is requiring the development of a new biology to accommodate them. **Body aches and pains** are very much part of the process of this evolution. Many will suffer unexplained dis-ease especially in the neck, shoulders and back. Headaches, temporary burning fits, and flue like symptoms are common. Utter fatigue is also very common and usually a temporary condition. Sometimes these symptoms will persist for a couple of weeks or more and then will spontaneously disappear. All these symptoms are the result of intense changes in your DNA that are awakening the new blueprint of your evolution. We will speak later of how you can manage these often debilitating experiences.

6.  Many of you will have experienced **changes in your sleep patterns**. It is likely that you will typically awaken many nights between 3.00 - 4:00 am. There's a lot of work going on within you, and it often causes you to wake up for a "breather." If you cannot go back to sleep, get up and do something rather than lay in bed and worry. It is a particularly good time for writing or meditating. You may go through **periods of intense dreaming**. These might include grotesque images, war and battle dreams, chase dreams or monster dreams. Often such dreams are experienced without fear but rather as an impassioned observer. You are literally releasing the old energy within, often from ancestral memories in your DNA.

7.  Commonly you may feel alone and removed from others. The desire to "flee" groups and crowds. You may have difficulty relating to others at times. These **feelings of loneliness** are also associated with the fact that only you can process what you are experiencing. The void within will

eventually be filled with the love and energy of your own spiritual consciousness that is awakening.

8. You may feel as if you have totally **lost your passion for life**, with little or no desire to do anything. Things that used to interest and inspire you, you no longer find much enthusiasm for. Try not to fight yourself on this. Take the time to do nothing. Sometimes to shut down is the only thing you can do to receive the new energies.

9. Many of your **relationships will** be in the process of **change**. There is commonly a strong feeling of **withdrawal from family**. You may feel privately quite differently about family members. There may be a distancing or an intolerance that you were not conscious of previously. Also you may experience a sudden change in your friendships. Friends will relocate, or there will be a gradual distancing, or even a sudden death. You are breaking the ties of old bonds and preparing for new friendships based on an entirely new energy contract without karmic attachments.

10. The Great Shift requires you to actually make changes in your life circumstance. Often this requires a **change in job or career, or geography, or even "life" partner.** As you change, things around you will change as well. It is not necessary to find the "perfect" job or career right now. You're in transition and you may make several job changes before you settle into one that fits your passion. Furthermore, for some it is enough to be prepared to make a change, and to put ones personal house in order, for a transformation to take place without any change in circumstance.

11. **Memory loss** is a particularly common experience. Difficulty in remembering what you did or who you talked to a day or sometimes just an hour before. You may have times of difficulty in accessing common words. Such loss is usually short term memory loss. At times you cannot even talk at all because you are simply unable to access much of anything. Sometimes you may be doing some task and be called away or distracted. When you come back you have no memory of what you were doing or where you have put something. It may be sometime later when you see what you had left and that you are reminded of what you were doing. You are in more than one dimension at a time, and going back and forth is part of the transition.

12. This memory loss is part of the **changes in your experience of time**. You are experiencing a disconnection with the linear time of past/present/future. The past disappears and becomes absorbed in the present moment. When you are engrossed in the present, time stops. Can 3 hours seem like 20 minutes? On the other hand, has time sped up for you? Are there less hours in the days, and are your years going faster and faster? Time appears to be accelerating as your experience of it contracts.

There are many other, sometimes dramatic symptoms people are experiencing and we have covered only a few of the most common. The world is heating up and so are you. It has little to do with the "Greenhouse effect". All the planets in our solar system are heating up, or changing shape or size, or both with the increased energy. Weather patterns reflect the changeability in ourselves and there is a curious matching if you observe closely. There are great upheavals occurring in the lives of everyone on this planet and we will see much suffering as people run this way and that, trying to avoid the decision that has to be made, or being unable to cope with the conditions. Look around you and see the desperateness of people's attempts to hide from themselves and life. Each searching for a security, belongingness, and happiness outside themselves that is more lasting. It is a futile endeavour and eventually leads to confusion, desperation and despair.

All this change is challenging much that had been seen as permanent in the world, and many are questioning their sanity. However, there will be no Armageddon. Instead, we are seeing an Apocalypse (a Greek derived word which means, "lifting the veil").

A new reality is emerging, and more fundamental, and often miraculous possibilities are emerging. The fact that the veil between the seen and unseen world is lifting is evident by growing numbers of people sensing and seeing phenomena that were previously experience only by psychics and mediums.

There is an amplification of the senses and increased sensitivity such as blurry vision, shimmering objects, seeing glittery particles, auras around people, plants, animals, and objects. Some report seeing formerly opaque objects as transparent. When you close your eyes, you are likely no longer to see darkness, but redness or even bright light. You may also see geometric shapes or brilliant colors and pictures when you close your eyes. Colors appear more vivid, the sky might look teal blue or the grass an amazing brilliant green. As you become more sensitive, you may see shapes or outlines in the air, especially when the room is almost dark. When your eyes are open or closed, you may on occasions see white or black moving shapes in your peripheral vision. Your vision is changing in many ways and you are experiencing new ways of seeing.

Your hearing senses may increase or decrease. You may have periods of hearing white noise in the head, beeps, tones, music or electronic patterns. Some hear water rushing, bees buzzing, whooshing, roaring or ringing. Others have what is called audio dyslexia with periods where you can't always make out what people are saying, as if you can no longer translate your own language. Some hear strange voices in their dreams, as if someone is hovering near them.

Enhanced senses of smell, touch, and/or taste are common experiences. You may be able to now smell and taste chemical additives in some foods. Other food may taste absolutely wonderful. For some people, these enhancements are both delightful and distracting. You might even smell the fragrance of flowers now and then out of nowhere.

There is nothing to fear in any of this. Surrender to it and let it come through. Listen and watch. Your senses are developing and are adjusting to new frequencies.

Your duty becomes very clear. Each of you who read this is growing in your spiritual understanding, your awareness. Know that there is liberation from all the suffering. Each must spend time, energy, and self discipline in learning to live in your own Light and sharing the Love that shines through with all others in your sphere of activity. It is by loving yourself, honouring the beauty that you are, and by example, that you will turn towards the Truth in yourself and that truth will set you free. The truth is not in elaborate theories or techniques. It is in the Heart of God and is reflected through your own heart in the capacity to radiate Light and share your Love through your actions, through the way you live.

It is not in great works that we find our growth and Divine expression but in performing the duty that we have at hand. Performing it with Love and to the best of our ability without thought of reward. Of course the rewards will come and you will find that you will always be given what you need. Opportunities will come for you to express more and more completely the fullness of your own potential. Everything you need to become the highest expression of yourself you will receive, you need only ask with the fullness of your intention and desire.

As you build the trust and confidence in your inner knowledge you will more fully experience the wonderful being that you really are. If you are sincere you will be given the help you need to move through all the obstacles that will be presented to you in order to strengthen your knowing. Guidance may come from a daily experience, a book, a friend or an opportunity to meet someone or do something new or make a change, but be assured that any sincere request for help in knowing who you really are will not go unanswered. Furthermore, because of this speeding up of evolution on the Planet Earth at this time, you will not have to wait long for the opportunity to move ever closer in your knowing of the Truth of your Spiritual Self and your part to play in the Great Plan.

We are all embarking on a great adventure. You feel the excitement in the air. Sometimes it's a little scary, sometimes it is frustrating because you know it is there but cannot see the vision of your own place in it very clearly. Be assured that no one who sincerely wishes to take the courageous step of moving to the sound of their own drum, will be left behind. There are millions like you around the globe. Brothers and Sisters of a Great Light who, hand in hand, are lifting their hearts to the stars and making the long journey home to the Truth of their own Being.

In a nutshell the world as we have known it is dissolving, fading into the new light that is radiating through all matter. If you choose to remain on this planet in this region and dimension of time and space then you must consciously, and of your own free will choose to, let go of old beliefs, take on the experience of knowing who and what you are to the fullest and to trust completely the unfolding of this next chapter of your existence, throwing yourself into it with courage, discernment, enthusiasm, and above all love.

# Chapter 2

# A New Point of View

Does matter exist if the human isn't looking? - Einstein

## A Quantum View of Reality

At the outset it must be accepted that however we describe our essential nature and the nature of creation we will always fall far short. How can we possibly describe and conceptualise Infinity or infinite creation? Look up at the stars at night. Stand and take in the possibility that space and this canopy of creation above you goes on forever and ever. Your mental mind cannot conceive of it and as you open to the possibility you begin to feel small and space engulfs you to the point that you feel a merging and a total loss of the sense of yourself as separate.

The left side of our brain, the mental mind, cannot conceive of anything without boundaries, but the right side can know truth without proof. Words cannot express it, but through our intuitive sensing we can experience something of creation, at least to some degree, that transcends our individualised sense of self. Any description of such realisation pales before the experience. And however we try to describe any sensory experience we feel "that's not it". How can you describe the experience of the colour red to someone who has never seen it. It is always something more than we can ever speak of.

Many of the scholars and rishis of Indian Vedic knowledge understood this and so after any sharing of their understanding of any truth of Nature or Creation would say "neti, neti", "That's not it". In saying this they were affirming their recognition that the truth was beyond the words they had shared. Lao Tse, the great Chinese Sage maintained that the Tao (the word used for the Limitless Consciousness and Energy of All That Is) that could be spoken of was not the Eternal Tao.

Given that our outline cannot be The Truth but that it paints a picture that represents a view of the Truth, let us outline some of the amazing insights quantum physics is giving us about our nature and potential.

## The New Reality

Welcome to the New Reality of the Quantum Universe. In a very real sense the whole spectrum of ideas and postulates that make up the fantastic world of quantum mechanics and physics is knowledge whose time has come. The Universe and physical reality has not changed but our knowledge of it has. The potentiality for realities totally different from that which humanity has believed for a long time has always been present but up until recently the consciousness of humanity has not been ready to receive it. As the new energies pour into your third dimensional reality, the division between this and other worlds is fading. The veil is thinning. Our vision is changing and thus new possibilities are arising. The "New Earth" for us is a new and fresh, expanded way of seeing reality, and this new way of seeing will reflect the reality postulated by quantum physics. Furthermore, it is a reality that holds amazing and miraculous creative possibilities for all of us.

So let us examine some of what a quantum view of reality and the Universe says and some of the implications this reality has on our knowledge of what we are and our potential. First, for me, the word "quantum" when referring to the new conception of the Universe seems rather clumsy and is often a bit daunting and off putting for those who do not consider themselves as scientifically inclined. Though the word "quantum" has quite specific and technical meaning and refers to the smallest discrete amount of any quantity in energy terms, I will refer to the reality to which

16

quantum physics points as the "New Reality". I will use this term advisedly knowing that the New Reality is not fixed, nor discrete, but encompasses a Universe of infinite experience and infinite possibilities beyond time and space.

## Science and Spirituality

Let us understand that science represents the epitome of the capacity of the human mind to comprehend the universe through imagination, deduction, logic and systematic analysis. The ideas of the quantum view of nature and the universe have been painstakingly derived through a mathematical and logical precision and critical observation and analysis. At the same time the conclusions of this science about the nature of the universe and our reality are remarkably similar to those that have been taught by mystics and metaphysicians throughout the ages. These great thinkers, however, reached their similar conclusions by careful and disciplined practice of "going within" and observing and understanding the universe through their own consciousness experience and intuitive knowing. The unifying of the two methods of knowledge has come about by science now recognising the star player in understanding Nature and the Universe, You. The primary conclusion is that it is consciousness that creates. God is back and we are all central players in Creation.

Now let us outline some of the major tenets of the science of the New Reality and the implications for the Universe and our power and place within it.

### 1. Unlimited Potential Throughout All That Is

Through the Atomic Age of the 20th century we have been taught to believe that energy is everything and that the Universe and everything in it is made of various particles which form atoms, which in turn forms all matter in the world we know so well. We have also generally believed and accepted that this world of matter, this objective world has existence independent of us; that the world of matter and objects is the world of substantial reality. That our own private world of feelings, desires, hopes, dreams and imagination have a secondary status. That they relate to impermanent and an unreliable and non universal reality.

It has been known for a very long time that this is not the way that things really are. Mystics have known it for ages and foremost thinkers in science have known it for almost 100 years. Creation, or the Source of All That Is, is often described from the New Reality perspective as a *zero point field*. It is an infinite field of nothing, or rather **No Thing.** It is a field of the unmanifest, whereas you can think of the world we know as a manifest world, a world that has been created and is observable. Creation thus consists of an unlimited and infinite potential of no-thingness. Even the vast stretches of 'space' are filled with unlimited possibilities including dimensions and realities as yet completely unknown to you or I.

### 2. Creation is in a Constant State of Change

Now this infinite field is in a state of constant change. There is no such thing as a vacuum. Space is not empty. Particles, energy, light are continually popping in and out of existence. Now you see it, now you don't. Change is the name of the game and there appears to be no beginning or end, nor limit to what can become manifest or return to no-thingness. In this field of potential of possibilities anything can be created.

### 3. Everything is Connected to Everything Else

Everything is connected to everything else. Two electrons created together are entangled. Send one to the other side of the Universe. Now do something to one and the other responds instantly. Either information is travelling infinitely fast or in reality they are still connected. They are entangled. And since everything was together in the beginning that means that everything is still touching. Space is just the construct that gives the illusion that there are separate objects. All energy, all matter, was bundled up in a miniscule ball that burst and now, even though everything is spread out across the infinite number of Universes, it is all still connected.

## 4. Non locality – No Time, No Space

Now as any energy or particle comes into existence it has the amazing property that it is in constant communication with all other particles in existence. This is known as non locality or non-separateness and says that a quantum entity eg electron, can influence another particle instantaneously over any distance without any exchange of energy or force. Whatever happens to it is instantaneously recorded in all particles throughout creation. There is no time lag for this communication and distance makes no difference, it is instantaneous. As such, time and space can be seen as illusionary.

Particles are not substantial bits of solid matter but rather waves of potentiality. These waves of potentiality are themselves determined but also their projection into actuality exhibits spontaneity.

In the quantum world, things are interconnected beyond the limits of space and time. Behind the classical world of separate material particles lies a world that is non-separable. In essence, a system of two particles is not two separate particles at all, but one non-separable potential which contains the possibilities for the manifestation of two particles. Similarly, a system of many particles is also united in the same way. Thus the whole universe is united in one wave of potentiality living in a vast space of unimaginable possibility. While the world appears to be a Many, the New Reality shows that it is fundamentally a One.

## 5. Holographic Universe

The universe is made up of things that are holographic. Holographic meaning that the information for a pattern occurring in a larger object will reoccur in all the smaller parts of that object. For example, every one of the many trillion cells that make up your body has the DNA pattern to reproduce your whole body with all its evolutionary history.

Any experience or thought is forever recorded throughout the universe. So in the Universe of your experience what is being said is that anything that happens to you is recorded instantly for anyone else to use within their experience. What holds your attention determines the potential influence you can have on anyone. Your view of what is possible contributes to the view that humanity as a whole has of reality.

### 6. As Above so Below

In taking this holographic view of reality we see also that because of the replicated patterning in all things it is not surprising that we now find that the laws that govern the Universe, Galaxies and the Cosmos are the same laws that explain and predict the characteristics of the smallest particles in existence.

The All is in the One and the One is in the all. The creative impulse is Love, infinite potential and everlasting change. That is the One and it is you. You too are made of the stuff of stars and as the solar system is expanding and being infused with increased energies of our Great Central Sun, a new template, a blueprint for new possibilities for this expansion, is being created in your DNA. and thus, throughout all that humanity is.

### 7. Reality is Defined by the Observer

Another profound discovery is that while energy travels like waves of potentiality it changes as soon as someone observes it. Instantly someone looks and applies focussed attention to an energy wave it changes into the discrete particles which constitute matter. When any object is not in your conscious awareness eg an atom, a chair, a cat, your own body, a thought in your brain, it is in a potential state. Only when you become conscious of it does it become actual and start behaving like something in particular.

In our New Reality, in order to account for the actual existence of anything physical, we are forced to recognize the existence of a nonphysical consciousness. The world is not just a bunch of inert matter, a collection of objects. There must also be a subject, a consciousness apart from objects, which is aware of them. Therefore it is the human consciousness present in individuals, you, that is what projects the potential to become actual.

There is an objective world, but it is not an actual world fixed in space and time. The true objective reality, the world that exists beyond the world that you actually see, is a potential world of possibility. Furthermore, that objective world of potentiality is non-separable—it is in a sense a single object. But out of this are manifest many countless relative worlds. Each world is appearing to different people in different places at different times. And from the different relative worlds, each mind-body never sees the whole potential reality but only a limited, actualized projection from one unique point of view, your own.

In addition behind this apparent proliferation of subjects (all the yous) and objects (all the things), everything is united and intricately interconnected. There is a world for you, a world for all your friends, a world for every plant and every animal, and even a world for the stars and planets and every single atom. Yet, in a deep and profound sense, these worlds are merely different projections of a single potential reality common to them all, a non-separable reality interweaving them all into a coherent whole. And at the center of each relative world is the one subject (God, the Creative Consciousness) uniting the worlds from the subjective side and making human relationships meaningful.

## 8. Consciousness Creates Reality.

Everything that apparently exists and has ever, or will ever happen, or exist, is a result of a consciousness that creates it, imagines it and intends it. Consciousness is behind all Creation. You and I create all that we know and could know and, it is through our conscious intention to accept for a moment in time some limits, that we have created the 3rd dimensional experience that we share. What we experience as our world is not independent of us as an observer but totally interdependent. How you view your world completely determines what your world will be. Human consciousness has accepted a reality by consensus and this is the world we have known.

The collective consciousness is now in the process of developing a new consensus based on the infinite potential to create that we are now bringing back into our conscious awareness. This new consensus will be aligned with the level of energy and light that is now pouring into all that you are.

## Amazing Implications for Who You Are

This New Reality provides an energy environment that is right here and now, veiled beneath the apparent reality of matter, determinism, and separation that is a now outmoded reality. The world is not made of hard matter. The world does not strictly follow deterministic laws. The world is not just a collection of separate parts. The world does not exist as a collection of objective entities, independent of observers. No, the world is not what we have thought it to be after all. Beneath this illusion lies a quantum realm where strange and wonderful things can happen. And this quantum wonderland is not some far off place, it is not some fiction. This is the world right here and now, a world that modern physics has helped to lead us to. A world that the Great Shift has given back to us to use for our greatest good, and the good of others. It is a power that we must now learn to use wisely, from the standpoint of our enlightened consciousness. The quantum world is here and now and becoming fully operative as we change our consciousness, our view of who we are.

Since, as we said earlier, so many of these ideas have been known in the scientific community for a long time and in the teachings of spiritual traditions for centuries, what makes them special now? After all they are only ideas that at best are changing our view of how our world works, and at worst are fantasy far removed from the world we at present experience and know.

Firstly, as we are experiencing the Consciousness Shift, the boundaries between energies and energy levels are disappearing. The way we are experiencing ourselves is changing and what used to work to balance and stabilize ourselves is no longer reliable or sufficient. You, your body, emotions, mind and environment are in a constant state of flux and you are continually having to make adjustments to bring yourselves back into a sense of balance, a sense of alignment with how you experience yourself and the new potentials you are beginning to experience, and trying to make sense of. This is unprecedented and raises all the issues that the quantum perspective of the New Reality seems to address.

Secondly, is the fact that, the effects of your shifting consciousness is requiring you to become fully engaged in your own change. That is, to become totally responsible for what happens to you and how you make the adjustments to maintain your own equilibrium in the ever changing state of your experiencing life. In other words, your waking up requires you to take up your own power to create. In order to do this your view of the world needs to match a truth of what is possible and a fuller understanding of who you are. Thus the New Reality is an idea which is now to have its time, both in terms of pointing to an energetic presence and also the readiness of the consciousness of humanity. Big things are about to happen and it is up to each one of us to explore, experiment, and deploy the energetic potentials in our Universe that are aligned with our deepest and most treasured ideals and imaginings, hopes and dreams.

## Conclusion

Taking what we have outlined so far. You and your reality are changing independent of any conscious effort on your part. The Consciousness Shift, brought about by the constant influx of new energies into the very makeup of who you are, is providing you with new and sometimes strange experiences and insights into yourself and your world. You are moving into a 5th dimensional experience.

This new evolutionary phase demands that you develop a different perspective on who you are and how you live. This new perspective is requiring that you gradually and fully accept an expanded vision. A position whereby you consciously take full responsibility for all that you experience and all you are creating in your world. You are in a state of change and transformation. A metamorphosis, like the butterfly coming out of its cocoon after a long period of a restrictive, and limited life as a caterpillar. Life is chaotic, turbulent, emotional, and confusing, interspersed with brief periods of stability and apparent quiet which help you to assimilate the changes.

At the same time the characteristics of the New Reality that we have briefly outlined tells us that the 5th dimension is a vast sea of infinite potential beyond time and space. It is a sea of constant movement of energies in and out of manifestation and in complete synchronisation. It is unlimited energies, light, and particles of infinite variety. Whatever is created in your universe requires a consciousness, a subject (eg you) to intend and experience it (any object or matter). Thus all things are and anything is possible. If it can be imagined or thought of it can be at any time, anywhere, as a potential to be created in form and experience.

Thus you have an unlimited power to create. The 3D world you know has been created by your intent which mostly, at this time, you are not conscious of. The world you experience is thus based on your thoughts, insights, hopes, fears, dreams and imagination. As you wake up to own the fullness of your consciousness you are waking to the fact that you are not a victim of your circumstances but a Master and Creator of them.

You are in the process of understanding your power to create and to create whatever experience you wish for, rather than be a victim of a consensus reality you have adopted from an accumulated and twisted history of fear, pain, guilt, doubt and unlovedness. Your liberation will come from changing your point of view to embrace all that you are and all that you can imagine that you can become, without limit and through your own choices.

Chapter 3

# Your Origin and Nature

Here is a story, a vision of a fantastic voyage. A voyage packed full of adventures. A story of unimaginable joy, and unlimited experience. It is your story and it is mine. It comes in limitless images and can be built on as each of us explores our potential, our imagination and the truth our magnificence.

## The Essence of You

We came from a point of light within the Mind of God, the Source of All That Is. We are conceived in Love and fashioned with Love. We are connected to all and there never has been, nor ever will be, separation for all is a grand unity, a magnificent blend of the energy of One. We are forever, and our journey is to experience All That Is in whatever forms or flavours we so choose.

Can you sense and imagine how awesome all this is? This is what you are no matter how limited you perceive yourself to be at this moment. Entertain, even for a moment, that all this is true. Take as a fantastic hypothesis that you might be Love Incarnate, of Unlimited Potential, Forever, and Never Alone, always connected to All That Is. What would you have to lose by taking the very next moment as it is, being totally open and allowing whatever will present itself to be, without any manipulation or preconception on your part. Everything would be an adventure, every experience would be embraced and lived fully.

Let us continue with the story. Let your imagination take you on this voyage as you read. Since you cannot imagine something that you have not experienced you must accept, with some validity, the truth of the voyage you will take.

You came as a spark of love consciousness from the Mind of Creation. Like an explosion of light and brilliant sparks from the centre of a potential firework of monumental proportions. The Big Bang of your creation. From the consciousness of Source you were "born" with innumerable Galaxies, Universes and dimensions lying before you. You have never known disconnection from Source. Aspects of you and your consciousness have explored the manifest realms, times and spaces of Creation. You, as it were, project aspects of yourself into opportunities for experiences and then, after long and incredible adventures withdraw that consciousness unto yourself to assimilate the fullness of the experiences into yourself and thus the Mind of God.

Think of the possible places and times you have frequented. Anything you can imagine, in some form or other you have experienced or will experience. As you are awakening in your current incarnation there are many things you are becoming aware of that previously you may not have taken seriously. Angels and fairies (and all kinds of nature spirits) are but two common examples. You cannot imagine these things if they have no basis in your consciousness or experience. Many of the fantastic creatures that have been generated in so many movies have not come from thin air. They originated from the movie creators imagination based on distant memories of experiences.

## The Creation of Your Current Self

Continuing the fantastic journey, you come to a time and place where you wish to experience in its fullest a third dimensional reality. You are drawn to a beautiful blue water planet in some far reach of a Galaxy. Some of you have been drawn just recently and some were attracted to this place in time and space a very long time ago. There is immense interest in this little planet at this stage in its evolution.

Countless beings are amassing with excitement because great changes are happening and new and unheard of transformations are taking place. Everyone wants to be here to learn and share in the unfolding experiences of the "New Earth". Many are present to lend their support and love. Some have desired so fervently to experience the fullness of third dimensional reality that they have incarnated. They have incarnated with the full knowledge that they would lose their memory of their connectedness, of their origin, and of their knowing. Thus we come to you and the present part of your fantastic journey.

## Becoming Human

In your infinite capacity for love and joy you projected a portion of your consciousness into form on Planet Earth. You created the thought seed of you in the first dimension. You projected a point of light that gathered unto itself a myriad of light particles (adamantine particles) and that focus of your consciousness then created an etheric replica of what you were to become and you projected a soul segment (an aspect of your consciousness) through the second dimension. The etheric replica settled around the foetus as it grew in your mother's womb. Gradually, as it formed you infused more of that portion of yourself that you were to project into the physical plane and it settled around the living conscious cells of the foetus as it grew. At birth the imprint of the consciousness on the gridwork that surrounds the form that you had projected, started to be assimilated into the form and as it did so you gained more of your individualised awareness and lost the memory of your greater Self, your consciousness of the connection to the Source of All That Is. As you entered through a vortex into the birth canal only a fragment of your original consciousness remained with you.

## Boundaries of the Human Experience

Everything you became in this lifetime you chose carefully from your point of greater awareness before ever taking the journey into physical form. You chose your parents, you chose difficulty or ease of birth. In choosing the time you were born you were able to choose a timing of the position of the planets that provided the best imprint for the characteristics and potentials you wished to develop and express in your life. That is, you chose the geometric configuration of the unique expression you were to become in your earth journey.

## Setting your Life Stage and the Players

Before you took your journey to this incarnation you gathered together with your real spiritual family. Those who you know so well, and are in total harmony with beyond the veil of your present life. Together you mapped out major events and major experiences you wished to have. Some of your family agreed to play parts in your life that are critical to lessons you wanted to learn. They may play a friendly or hostile role but all agreed to play their part out of their great love for you. Someone in your life may be set to initiate strong feelings in you of being a victim. This same soul on the other side may love you so much that they have agreed to appear as your enemy. These players are all part of your Family from Home, where the unity and Godliness of all is unquestionable. In agreement you asked these players to act as a mirror to any unlovedness you feel about yourself. Any self-loathing that has become part of the separation and fear that you experience is then mirrored back to you through the loving act of another, who themselves will be in the veil of illusion of their own separateness and unlovedness. You are now staging an amazingly intricate play, a play so real to the players that each has become lost in their own role. You have become unconscious of the major part of who you are.

How could you have a full experience if you knew it was a play from the beginning?

## Personality

Choosing the time you are born you also choose the kinds of forces and directions which you will prefer to work with in order to maximise the benefits of the life tasks you have decided to work on. This is the kind of character you will be in your life play. Together we refer to these characteristics as your personality. These traits determine how you will express yourself. They, to a large extent, determine the way you process the information you receive. For example, male energy focus tends to process information in a serial way, that is, one bit at a time, the size and scope of the picture can be vast but the processing is sequential. The female energy focus tends to result in processing information in parallel, whereby the connections between all bits of information are available all at once and so any connection between any bit is possible. Thus whether you are actually male or female you tend to have some preferred mode of operation.

Your personality will also reflect how you will tend to react to situations. For example, when presented with a new situation an introverted person is likely to first observe and take the situation in before reacting, while an extroverted person may be more inclined to react first and then later take the response in and mull it over in their mind.

Further, your personality traits determine how you will express yourself. Some people express themselves far more from a sensing and feeling standpoint while another's preferred mode may be thoughtful, and systematic. Some are much more at home with their intuitive creative expression while others are most at home with a logical and practical approach to life. None of these traits are better than any other they are merely characteristics of the expressing of the viewpoint you, as an individual being, bring to your world.

Each has come with a gift for all and each is in the process of discovering this gift which is your major mission for the life you are developing in the New Reality.

## Forgetting

As you incarnated you forgot who you truly are. You forgot that you are love incarnate, that you are created within and from the Source of All That Is which is All Love. Further, you forgot that you are forever connected to All That Is and cannot be separated. You are indivisible and indestructible, whole and united. This forgetting at birth has been referred to as being 'born in sin'. The original meaning of 'sin' was 'off the mark'. Thus to be 'born in sin' is to be born not knowing who you are. There is no negative connotation. It is merely a statement of fact that you have forgotten yourself. The purpose of life therefore, is to wake up to the full truth of yourself. Your lovingness, your wholeness, your everlastingness and your belongingness to All That Is. All this while living in a third dimensional reality.

## Free will

As you descended and were born into your new life experience, you began to take your Free will. Having freewill has meant that your life is governed by the choices you make within all the conditions and opportunities that present themselves to you. You are playing a game of hide and seek. The truth of who you are is hidden subtly inside and calling you in times of quiet, and you are presented with a 3D reality where everything that calls you to action appears to be outside yourself and very noisy. You are continually being challenged to choose between your guidance system and being directed from the subtle feelings within, or the gross pressures from without. Your life is about the choices you make and in fact, from the point of view of who you really are, there can be no wrong choices because all actions lead to experience from which you can learn.

## Development of Ego

An essential part of having taken on a 3D experience of yourself are deep feelings of being separate from other beings, of being disconnected. At the same time in developing an identity, you have within you a need to protect who you think you are against attack. You take on your ego experience which gives you a sense of being an individual with an existence independent of other entities in your world. Your ego is the divisible force which protects the survival of who you think you are. It acts to protect, against all odds, the destruction of your sense of self as a separate individual.

## Birth Trauma

Birth is seldom without trauma up to these current times, where all of humanity is in the process of totally clearing the pain of the past. Not only is it a shock to that part of your consciousness, the soul fragment that has incarnated, to start loosing memory of your Source, but also fear imprints need to be taken both in the womb from the mother and also from early childhood experiences. Fear and sense of separation have been a part of the human experience for so long. So the birth and early experiences you have taken on provide the opportunity for an exact experience of a self-chosen reality. You are not a victim of circumstance but a Master of choice. Every human has taken on the experiences of their life at this time in order to release the pain and suffering of the past and fulfil the mission of bringing some unique gift to earth for all to share. You have chosen to be here to experience the budding of a human being free of the past, and everyone has chosen to transmute and clear a piece of the shadowed past totally, as the Earth moves fully into the fifth dimension. No matter how it may appear, not one person is in truth a victim. All, no matter how apparently conscious or asleep to who they are at this time, are performing the profound and loving service of removing the karma of the shadow of ignorance for all time.

## Karma and Dharma

Within the framework of the life you have built are two pressures that move you to action. One is karma.

Now karma or the Law of Karma is a most benign attribute of your life. It does not refer to a law of retribution, whereby if you do something wrong then something must return to you in kind in the future. Karma refers to the reality of the causal effects of the play you are enacting and have set in motion. Your karma will be the pressures that life circumstances will place on you continually until you turn within and accept the truth of who you are. Karma is the built in conditions for your path to enlightenment, your way Home. Karma provides you with a mirror, through the life circumstances you place in your pathway, in order to show you who you are being in the present moment. If you are asleep to something that holds you back from a realisation of yourself, then a life circumstance will arise to get your attention and jog your memory.

The second pressure is known as dharma and is often thought of as ones Duty. Dharma comes from within and it is a constant pressure to fulfil yourself, to be happy, to be active and to express the energy of being yourself. Dharma requires you to discover and express your talents and abilities. To give your gifts to the world. To make your mark.

Consequently, you incarnate into an experience whereby these two pressures act on you in order that you grow and make the most of your life. Through life you are involved in a balancing act between the pressures of life circumstances that are calling you to be who you truly are and the pressure within for the need to express who you truly are, karma and dharma. Your life circumstances, your relationships, will always mirror back to you what you truly and deeply think and feel about yourself. This is the way you set the whole thing up before you came here and these are the conditions you decided to live under in order to maximise your chances of getting the most out of your experience.

## God Finding a New Perspective

Given the restrictions we place on our soul in order to have an Earth (3D) experience is it any wonder that those on the other side who watch our progress honour us so deeply? How courageous it is to come here and experience the pain of separation and deep feelings of threat to our survival and wellbeing. How gallant to act through love, to come into this reality and change it by knowing the losses personally, and by transcending the experiences through love and forgiveness of self and all others.

Now it is time to transform that reality through taking back the truth of who you are. Understanding and forgiving everything that has been. Letting it all go. Especially, forgiving everything you have done or been a part of. Seeing it as a chapter in your fantastic voyage. A wonderful gift of learning to become One with your true Self.

The journey is only just beginning because as you begin to find yourself you realise more that there is no end to the possibilities in human affairs and what can be created. What kind of world do you want in your experiencing of freedom and mastery? As you take fully your rightful place alongside Mother Earth what kind of heaven on earth can you conceive of? You create the Path, which leads to your own destiny. Dig deep my friends for there are many seeds you can plant and you will be very surprised how quickly they can grow.

Humanity is at last waking up to the infinite possibilities that were once only a distant dream. The stronger you envisage your dreams the more likely they will manifest not only in your reality but in the hearts of others. We are all on this fantastic voyage together and, however it manifests, it will be a shared endeavour. The conscious freewill participation of you in your voyage will contribute to the expanding consciousness of humanity and makes available your own unique journey for the benefit of all humanity. Your journey and your growth add unique flavours to human consciousness, a unique blending of energy and light, and thus enhances the possibilities for our life together. The combined effect of the millions of people on this planet, who are taking full ownership for their own voyage, has assured that a new reality consensus is now in the process of unfolding. Come join us as we explore the limitless possibilities of experience together. Come join in the next adventure in the New World we are creating. It will be. All it needs is your sincere intention, then know, as you walk your journey that, So It Is.

You are an essential aspect of the One Consciousness. You are God finding a new aspect, a new point of view, through your experience. The unique perspective you will find, through discovering what is true and what works to bring you love, joy, empowerment, and fulfilment, will contribute to the knowledge record for all to gain from.

# Chapter 4

# Your Human Past

In this present lifetime we have come into embodiment with much to contend with. The pressure of the ages is upon us and as we have seen, the time has come for earth and humanity to shake off the old energy accumulation and memories of the past history, to clear away any blockage and disease in the mind and hearts of our consciousness, and to identify fully with our Divinity.

Some understanding of what you have been and what has been carried forward into how you experience yourself in this present time will help empower you in your journey to remember. You are waking up, becoming fully conscious of your own beauty and grand design and nature. You have lived in the shadow of yourself for a very long time and now it is time to step into the light, into your own radiance.

## Collective Human Unconscious

There was once a time on earth when humans lived much longer lives (600-1000 years or more). During a lifetime there was more than enough time to have all the experiences a soul desired, and to fulfil every purpose and mission that you set yourself. As humanity moved further into this physical density, the veil of forgetting our origin increased and the task of becoming totally conscious of who we are became increasingly difficult. Thus people began to pass over without having processed all that was necessary for 'enlightenment' and any miscreation of thoughts, and actions began to accumulate in the collective human unconscious. These unprocessed energy thought forms had to be dealt with by those who incarnated. They were imprinted as memories in the DNA and so subconscious experiences and patterns of reaction developed as part of the soul contract and experience of an individual. Fixed patterns of belief and the attendant rituals became part of the cultures of various societies in an attempt to express and to free these blocked energies.

While you each have your set of dramas that you are living through, there is also a Grand Play being enacted by the whole of humanity. We are all connected in a great unity.

## Consensus Reality

Every human being lives in a world constructed of their own thoughts and beliefs. Thoughts are the stuff from which all we see is created. Our thoughts are coloured by the biology we inherit because the racial memories are imbedded in the DNA, developed from the experiences of those who have gone on before, our ancestors. In each incarnation we take on cultural patterns of seeing and thinking through the language we are taught. Each language has its own biases. Ways of seeing the world and particular priorities the culture has for noticing, constructing and interpreting their environment. For example, the Maoris living in New Zealand lived in a land that was predominantly evergreen forest. Thus in their language there are several different words for 'green'. They learned to make distinctions and thus see differences in their environment that in our modern English language we do not need to make so do not see those differences.

The cumulative record of all the different human experiences as a whole goes to make up a reality that we can tap into and this becomes the consensus reality, the reality that we appear to hold in common. It is in fact what the Indian Vedic teachings refer to as 'Maya', the world of illusion, or more accurately, appearance. The consensus reality, the one we seem to share, does not really exist. It is only a collective representation of reality and we are now moving into a time and space experience where it is totally unstable because it is in the process of major change as we find ourselves anew and redefine what will be "out there".

## Ancestry

The biological bubble we have taken on is not only a unity of trillions of cells. Each cell contains a library of the history of humankind. Each cell has identical DNA which provides a record of all that has gone before. Your family tree is vast with millions of ancestors having contributed to the record you hold. All the experiences, joys and sorrows, struggles and pain, knowledge and talents are imprinted there within you. Any one of your experiences in this lifetime can trigger a whole series of ancestral memories. This is why you can experience strong and sudden emotions that are often out of proportion to the events in your life that triggered them. This is quite understandable really, when you consider the accumulated hardship and suffering your ancestors have endured.

Some of the experiences of the past have been learned so well that they have formed deep impasses in our responses to life now. For example, the pain and terror of the destruction of Atlantis has made its mark on the collective unconscious of generations of our ancestors. Thus we have imprinted on our DNA, the idea that taking our own spiritual truth, the power of who we are, could be very dangerous to our survival. We should not trust our own motivations. The fear of total annihilation underlies our fear of taking our own truth. You do not trust yourself to be a creator. Thus you have placed a guardian to stop you from overriding all else with a spiritual arrogance. It is a lesson well learned but that still has to be cleared in order for you to find the courage to be yourself.

## Archetypes

Coming out of the accumulated memories of the collective unconscious are universal patterns of feeling and behaving that speak in the language of the subconscious. These are referred to as archetypes and represent typical responses to life situations that have been repeatedly experienced by our ancestor. These are qualities and habits of responding that are not individually acquired but inherited, inborn forms of perception and apprehension, which predetermine how we are likely to see and react to other people and to particular situations.

An example of an archetype is one of the Giver. A Giver is driven by self worth that is measured by how well they have served others. There can be a constant emptiness, with little understanding of personal emotional needs despite an understanding of those same needs in others. When service is given and not appreciated, guilt can overwhelm such a person. If the service required is too demanding, the Giver no longer performs with a smile, but rather with a begrudging, and disgruntled attitude. Others paradoxically interpret this as selfishness. A Giver at the highest expression, however, learns to exercise responsible choice with consideration of their own needs and feelings.

You have chosen to take on a number of these archetypes and play them out in your life in order to get a full understanding of the limits of your expression from a 3D point of view.

## Shadow

Each archetype has a light and shadow side to it. The shadow is the opposite of the ego image we consciously have of ourselves. It often contains qualities that you do not like to identify with but that you possess nonetheless. The shadow side holds us back from what we want. It manifests itself in us as being stuck, depressed, and fearful. The light side of the archetype connects us with the perfect blueprint of our soul, our higher essence and purpose. We will discuss this further in the next chapter.

## Past Lives. Experiences and Lessons

You have made this journey into the third density many times. For some it is numbering in the many hundreds. Each time you incarnated you gathered experiences, primarily directed towards gaining an intimate understanding of yourself, your limitations and opportunities within this vibrational frequency. You have developed many skills and talents which at present you are not aware of. You also have experienced extremes of joy and pain in the huge array of the life circumstances you found yourself in. You have accumulated a magnificent reservoir of knowledge based solidly on the apparent trials and tribulations of the struggle between self-expression and the restrictions you set up for yourself. Such restrictions were necessary for this is the nature of a finite reality. Each experience has contributed to your knowing, to your courage and daring. The feelings you now have about how the world is not as it is supposed to be, your deepest feelings of enough is enough, are based on a long history whereby you know the pain and suffering of the world because you have been there and experienced it. You know the potential of humanity because you have seen it countless times in other journeys and you have experienced your own strength to rise above almost impossible odds. You have experienced first hand, through your own lives, how low and degraded you can go and how high in self-expression you can rise.

You bring all this with you now, and though you may not remember any of it, it will appear as faint murmurings of your own potential and the potential of others. "There must be much more, I know there is". It will emerge as strong patterns of responding which seems to hold you back and remind you of past suffering. It will emerge as feelings of longing for something lost and remind you of joy. It will appear in images and dreams of days gone by that are familiar and rousing. It will remind you of lessons learned and forewarn you so that you can make more appropriate choices in your present journey.

## Power Mongering

A long and repeated history has played itself out in your past lives and the dramas you have enacted. You have inherited the imprints of these patterns in your DNA and they are being played out in the lives of all humanity at this present time. The past of humanity, your past, is saturated with experiences of a sense of powerlessness and a quest for personal power.

Your personal power has been continually eroded through your relinquishing it to external and internal pressures from others. You have unknowingly given away your power through fears and doubts in yourself.

### 1. External Conditioning and the Loss of Life Force

Fundamental to the human experience has been the sense of powerlessness. People come into this world totally dependent on others for their survival and thus soon learn who has the power and how to get it. Children have been taught that they are powerless by themselves and need to look to others for the source and experience of their sense of power and control. Different cultures and societies have looked in different directions but the process has been virtually the same. Your human past has conditioned you very thoroughly to look beyond yourself for the source of your own power.

In reality what has happened is that, in childhood, through fear conditioning of all kinds, control and direction of the very life force, the Chi, of a child becomes vulnerable to the intents of other. Thus began all the human manipulations that fundamentally meant that to gain this vital power, the Chi, because you did not have enough, you had to take it from someone else.

Because you did not have confidence in yourself and who you were, for countless lives you gave away your Chi to others. In being taught to confuse the boundaries between yourself and others you became vulnerable to the needs of others. The lack of boundaries has meant that anyone you 'let in" through any emotional need whatsoever, started to have access to your Chi. Many people have known how to manipulate others to gain this life force. It is what so often makes fame. A person is usually only influential to the extent that others give them some of their Chi.

Most of this game of power gain and loss is so well established that it is lodged deep in your subconscious whereby mostly you are neither consciously aware of the many subtle ways you give your Chi away or take someone else's. Sometimes, however, it becomes fairly obvious. For example, healers and caregivers often feel very depleted after prolonged or frequent client sessions. Being open to give they have not defined their boundaries enough to offer detached love. They have merged their boundaries with that of another through their own emotional needs and allowed the other to take their Chi rather than allowing their clients to take back their own life force.

For centuries at the personal, family, societal and national level people have attempted to steal the life force from others through the manipulation of fear and the imprisoning of freedom. You will see it being played out when, in a relationship, one person seems to thrive while the other shrivels up. You will feel it in the presence of certain people who exude a need to dominate or a person who is playing "poor me". In the former the experience is like a great hand attempting to crush or pull something from you and in the latter like a sucking, sickly feeling. The memories of these sensations have become instinctive.

Because of your need to be certain and your lack of trust in yourself you are in the habit of looking to powerful others to give you the clues to your own power. Our history is littered with big as well as countless small events, whereby our ancestors have followed strong leaders to conquer and steal the Chi of others. Thus the feeling that someone else has the knowledge is very strong in us and we continue to look outside for the answers. Listening to others truth and disregarding our own is so second nature to us.

## 2. The Dark Voice Within

As we have mentioned, over the long history of our forgetfulness humanity has accumulated a vast reservoir of unconsciousness based on belief systems that deny our power. Our distant memories are littered with untruths about the untrustworthy and the shadowy nature of humans. Because you come into the world with a reflection of this past you easily take on the distrust of yourself and what may be lurking in the depths of your unconsciousness. Through the ages our religious institutions have been quick and very effective to play on and feed the fears and doubts we have about our essential worthiness.

The whole idea of "the devil' is a very good example of how the shadowy unconscious has been played with. It has been a way to externalise the inner feeling of distrust of the shadow side of ourselves. Interestingly the word 'devil' spelled backward is 'lived', perhaps pointing to the fact that you are not fully living while the shadow in you remains unintegrated and unillumined.

Beings and entities from many dimensions, who do not have physical bodies and who, for one reason or another, quest for the power that humans possess, have always been attracted to the human condition. Though they cannot take form they can certainly gain a sense of power and control through any influence they can have on a human life. Such influence is gained through the nefarious attempt to project thoughts that play on the fear and doubt of the unsuspecting.

Hearing an inner voice, whisper in the ear has been part and parcel of the human experience. Through doubt in self many a horror has been enacted through the influence of these so called "dark forces". Their influence has contributed significantly to the shadow aspects of the human drama. Much of your own dramas have been the result of doubting yourself and listening to those voices that have played on your fear and paranoia.

Much of the human history of 'evil' has played itself out through listening to the shadow voice of self. As humans, we have been so afraid of owning and embracing all that we are, that we have perpetuated the notion that the inner voice cannot be trusted, that it is evil and will destroy ourselves and others. Again, interesting enough the word 'evil' backwards spells 'live' and even more significant is the fact that it is also an anagram of 'veil'. By not owning the shadow self, the other half of ourselves, we cannot live fully and we perpetuate the veil between ourselves and our truth within, our Higher Self.

The 'negative' entities no longer hold our power and are fading into the nothingness from which they came. Dissolving at an ever increasing rate as humanity is overcoming their fears and replacing beliefs systems that have said that we are less than Divine, less than the creators of our own destiny.

Humanity, you and I, have had a history of hearing the voice within that has lead us in a direction that was against our highest good and the highest good for others. The past has caught up with us. It is time for you to start fully listening to your Higher Truth within and to overcome the trepidation of the whispers from your own and your ancestors past shadowy experiences.

# Conclusion

Taken together all the past experiences that we appear to have taken on presents us with a seemingly daunting task if we are to heal it all. Recognising that we are in a time where all the past has risen to be cleared then it is no wonder you feel swamped and confused by what is happening to you and what you feel you should do to be in balance, at peace and happy.

All your experiences (the past) you have chosen. They do not define the worth of you. They have nothing to do with your worthiness or otherwise. They are simply experiences from the choices you have made from limitless potential. No choice is **the right** choice. As soon as you awaken to the realisation of the amazing game you have been playing with yourself you become free to choose. You can make the decision that enough is enough. You can choose to take your own power instead of being a victim and holding on to beliefs that make you feel lesser than you really are. The layers of past will begin to drop away.

No one is given more than they can handle. Put another way, you have only taken on in this lifetime what your inner being knows you have the potential to master. An important step to the solution is not trying to achieve it all at once. Trust is the key. Trust in yourself to be able to handle what comes to you in a step by step process. Trust in the universe to provide you with the circumstances and information to make the choices that lead you forward in your journey. Trust in developing a new, open and freer way of interpreting your world. And Trust in the loving self you are becoming, you are remembering.

Remember, every time you see the archetype you are playing out and understand it as that, you free yourself from its patterns of behaving and feeling. Every time you understand what your relationships or your dreams are telling you about yourself, and appreciate the lesson learned, you make it easier for someone else to do the same. The whole of humanity, no matter how apparently asleep, is involved in this process of releasing the past patterns of unknowing.

Many of the old paradigm structures of humanity's past, including fear based institutions of control and hierarchical governments, could not change before now because the consensus reality did not support it. The consensus reality is formed by individuals over time, each person shaping it by how they view the world. People's views include countless belief systems held within their DNA. These beliefs include those inherited from your ancestors many generations back, those formed in past lives, those taken from the mass consciousness, and those formed in the current life. All of these reside in the subconscious and out of ordinary awareness.

To change the consensus reality requires that a sufficient number of people (a critical mass) change their world view, from the inside out, and then apply the new view to actions in the world. This change occurs in one person at a time, yet the inner change of just one person can affect many other people.

The great news is that the critical mass for a new reality in the consciousness of humanity has already occurred. No longer need we fear for the survival of the planet. There are enough people (numbering in the millions) who have turned to begin taking their own power of love with directed intent, such that a momentum has gathered for all to take advantage of. Your task is to heal the past through your loving intent. Seeing and feeling life as a wonderful journey and valuing the gifts of understanding that you are gaining.

# Chapter 5.

# Your Present Experience

## The Task of Waking Up

The Shift in consciousness and the new energies entering our planet are moving you to your very core. The change is raising the level of consciousness on the planet at this time so that you can merge your mastery of the 3$^{rd}$ dimension with the fifth and even sixth dimensional realities. You are waking up to a fuller and more magnificent You. Uncontrolled emotions and behavioral patterns, some of which have been suppressed for many life times are rising up. They must be released to enable you to merge with the incoming consciousness.

Every single thought ever created is still woven within the fabric of human consciousness. Your thoughts create, absolutely. This is what composes a Conscious Grid that ultimately defines the limitations of your perception. Every individual personality is going to be revealed. You are experiencing isolated, seemingly real events in the unified field of reality in which everything is occurring at the same time. Your life is simply an event in your own time/space continuum, which is a part of the much larger whole. Likewise, the universe is undefined and limitless, and also it is infinitesimal and unique. As above, so below. As with the universe, so with you.

All the pain that was experienced during the destruction of Atlantis is currently being released and felt by every human being that had an experience there. The emotional response to this frequency is affecting everyone and everything around them.

49

All of this is being released on a global level. With every breath you take, you are exchanging cells with all of those who are now or have ever occupied this dimension. Perhaps this can begin to explain where all those strange thoughts and dreams about past lives and even parallel lives are coming from. It is not madness but the universal human memory unfolding at an accelerating rate.

## Clearing the Past- Karmic Imprints

What all this means is that you are waking up to all you are. You are becoming totally conscious. You are learning to be fully responsible for what you are and what you create. That responsibility means that you are taking back fully all your power and knowing and learning to be aware and present every moment.

It is the task of each one of us to take full charge of ourselves, and through love, patience, and acceptance, transmute and clear the past as it arises within us. We will heal the past patterns simply through the recognition, acceptance and integration of the daily experiences we will have. Through the compassion and understanding we have for what comes up in us and our reality.

As you read on please remember three things. Firstly, you are not alone in all the clearing of the past that is necessary. Every single person on this planet is bringing in a special contribution they can make towards the understanding, experience and healing of the past. We are One human family and no matter how conscious or not a person is of their responsibility in becoming a creator, each has a piece of the whole puzzle to complete the total transformation that will occur.

Secondly, you do not have to know anything in particular in order to play your part. What you are learning is that whatever you think, whatever you feel, and whatever events and situations come in your life, everything is in order. Everything you need in order to make your journey has been given to you by your own Being (Higher Self) and will be given to you step by step. All you need to do is to face your days with a positive expectancy and learn from what comes. Learn from your reactions and feelings. Learn from your thoughts and insights. And wherever and whenever you can, to bring your loving understanding to bear on it. Do so to the best of your ability and understanding and all will be well with you. You cannot fail.

Thirdly, many of you have been consciously searching and sifting through your life experiences for many years. You have been on a very long journey of years in this lifetime and have grown tired and often very disillusioned with your efforts and the world you have seen. Your body has taken on various conditions that seem to be impossible to shift. You have taken on many beliefs about the inevitability of the breakdown of your body with age. You may well feel that it is perhaps too late for you to make the changes that are required and that somehow you should have done better than you have.

Know that there is no judgment of failure or wrongness in what has occurred for you. You are the only one that judges yourself. No one has 'missed the boat'. You have not failed because you have been so often stuck and feeling far from where you would like to be. All your past efforts to make changes in yourself and this world have contributed to where the human consciousness is now. Someone had to prepare the ground for the changes that are occurring now. You chose to come here ahead of Shift and form a bridge from the third to fifth dimensions. You had to do it almost as a blind person, on your own, while for years carrying the pain of the past along with you. Your courage, your dedication, your refusal to give in completely to the 'mad' world has created the foundations on which the successful transition for so many can now take place. None of your life has been wasted. Now it is time to rest a while with the angels (without dying) and allow the healing of you to take its course. It is your time to choose the simple things that you enjoy. It is now time to taste the sweetness of your love, and understanding of God and your compassion for those around you who are waking up. The big task has been completed, thankyou. Now it is your time.

With these three things in mind we will examine some of the characteristics of how you have typically experience this 3D reality and some points of view that will take you beyond the apparent limiting conditions that you experience.

## The Duality Energy Plane

The third dimension, this reality you know so well, is a vibratory energy realm of comparison, contrast and polarity. It is referred to as the world of duality. You have experienced life primarily through a filter of duality. As children you grow to view the world through your language. How you and your world appear is predominantly coloured by the way it has been described to you and the internalisations of those descriptions through the colour of language of the culture you were born into. You may have developed your own unique flavour but nevertheless your view of reality is mostly determined by the belief systems that you hold. These belief systems come from how you have been treated and spoken to and they are internalised as your inner dialogue.

Duality creating is the fundamental characteristic of language. To speak and share about any characteristic of our world you have had to make distinctions and contrast between elements. Language and words are dichotomy producing. For example, to understand 'on" you have to compare it with 'off'. It has no meaning otherwise because it has no referent. To understand the idea of 'me' there has to be a 'you'. To understand 'black' there has to be 'white'. 'Love' and 'hate', 'greed' and 'generosity', 'war' and 'peace' and so on for anything you can speak of. There are **two sides to everything** that can be spoken about.

The mental mind (your internal dialogue) thus develops with this classification system with each distinction we make including both sides in the equation of experience. This is all very well and necessary but the problem arises because you have made this your reality with many preferences for one side of distinctions and in doing so you have lost touch with your experience of yourself and your world. Your internal dialogue is biased by the belief systems that you hold. These belief systems have been conditioned and programmed to have erroneous and self destroying outcomes, because they leave half of what you are out of your legitimate experience. For example, a person who does not feel good about themselves seeks to depend on others for their sense of approval and self-esteem. The half they have left out is there own power to initiate their own sense of worth through the direct experience of competence in what they do. Often there are many layers to the distinctions (duality influence) you typically make. In our example, low self-esteem can come from believing that the preferences others have for a happy life are the ones you should take on rather than your own. The limiting belief dichotomy therefore is that others choices are better than your own.

It is fair to say that all the pain and distress we experience is the result of the false distinctions we make and then take on as if they stand for something real, distinct and tangible. They become our identity. We become what we think and we think what we have been lead to believe. So perhaps your present, what you experience now, is only half the story? Could it be that by stepping out of the world of duality, by embracing both sides of yourself, something grande will happen? Could it be that by understanding all that you have been, through acknowledging the other side of you, that the whole is greater than the sum of its parts, far, far, greater? You are much, much more than you think you are at present.

## Two Sides of the Brain

Your experiencing of duality has its origin in the brain. You have two brain hemispheres which are physically separate from each other though they do communicate. Each hemisphere processes information differently, each side thinks about different things. They focus on different things and in a sense they have different personalities.

Your right hemisphere is totally concerned with this present moment. It is focussed exclusively on what you are experiencing right here, right now. It thinks in pictures and it learns kinesthetically, through the movement of your body and the sensing of energy all around and within you. It can handle multiple energy streams simultaneously through all your sensory systems. It then can give you enormous collages of what this present moment looks like, what it smells like, and tastes like, what it feels like, and what it sounds like. You are an energy being connected to the energy all around you through the consciousness of your right hemisphere. From the point of view of your right brain everyone is an energy being connected to one another through consciousness as one human family. Right here and right now we are one family of humankind on this planet. We are here to connect with all we experience and make the world a place of exploration and joy. Viewing from your right brain you would see that we are all beautiful, perfect and compete in the timeless, spaceless place of this instant.

Your left hemisphere tells you a very different story. Your left brain thinks linearly and methodically and in terms of polarities as we have described. Your left hemisphere is all about the past and the future. It is designed to take that multifaceted collage of the present moment from the right brain knowing and start picking out details, and details, and more details about those details. It compares and contrasts everything. It then categorises and organises all that information, sorts it into types based on similarities and differences, associates it with everything in the past that you have ever learned, and projects into the future, classifies all the details of all that might possibly happen based on the details it has stored from its past recording. It puts priorities and sorts information according to the strength of the emotional experiences (the emotional charge) associated with it. It forms well defined and often inflexible boxed files of information after repeated exposure to an experience.

Very importantly, your left hemisphere thinks in language. It is that ongoing brain chatter that connects you and your internal world to your external world. It is that little voice that says to you "Don't forget to put the rubbish out tomorrow". It is that voice that reminds you when you have to go for an appointment. Most importantly it is that voice that says to you "I am". As soon as you first realised "I am" as a child you became separate. You became a single physical, individualised, separate being from the flow of energy around you and from the deeper and essential side of you.

## Living in the present

Now it is obvious wherever you are, whatever the reality you live in you can only experience the present. The future is only a potential to come, and the past is made only of your memories and how you have coloured them among the many possible colour combinations you could have used. You can only know for certain what you are experiencing right now. And in this next minute what is happening now. This is where your knowing is. Our outline of the basic characteristics of the two sides brain gives you a most fundamental key to release the hold of your analytical mind. That to really start to live more fully and consciously and realistically you need to experience more of what your right brain is giving you and to drop the one-sided dominance of the left. To literally step to the right. To get out of your own way so that you can begin to more fully and deeply live according to your inner nature and not by a system of internalised rules that maintains your feelings of powerlessness, pain and confusion.

As you read on in this book all the tools that will be suggested, all the ideas for developing a different point of view, all the reminders will point towards how to more fully get out of your own way. To live more in the present and to let go of the memories of that which no longer serves your highest purpose.

## You are what you identify with.

Stepping beyond the world of duality is learning to heal the memories that hold you to a life that you no longer choose to identify with. The power that this old reality has over you is that at present its dominance in your consciousness keeps reminding you that you are not where you wish to be. The simple solution, but the most difficult, is to start living more in the present, since it is the only place you can really be. But you have to do this with a new identity. An identity that is more authentic, that is more really what you choose consciously, what you prefer to be.

We are what we identify with. A person who is very concerned with the things they 'own', their car house, designer gear, etc, will invest a great deal of the personal energy into their material life. When their possessions are threatened by loss or damage, their reaction is one as if the loss or damage was to themselves personally. A couple who invest themselves in their relationship are threatened when their investment does not keep pace with other aspects of their development. Scholars or clergy are threatened when their theories and beliefs are criticized. Each person defends the reality they have built. Their definition of themselves is determined by what they believe, what belongs to them, be it ideas, opinions, people, or material things. Threaten any of these things and a person will react as if their life is being threatened. This makes perfect sense since all that we have to give is our energy and intention and if it is invested in things outsides ourselves those things become a part of us. Their survival becomes our survival.

You are what you think. Your thoughts define you. While your conscious experience is primarily based on your thoughts then you are imprisoned by only one side of yourself, your left brain.

So the trick is to learn to redefine what you identify yourselves with and to choose consciously where your attention will go. Your **energy flows where your attention goes**. Identifying with the deeper, more permanent, expansive, and loving side of yourself, your priorities, your intentions, and your attention changes. Your energy starts to move in more creative directions of your own choosing.

## The Death of the Subconscious Mind

The new energies entering your body have loosened the subconscious beliefs and thoughts. Previously humankind has been able to invest a major part of their energy system in suppressing unwanted and fear based thoughts below the level of immediate awareness. A great deal of energy is required to maintain the denial of thoughts that we cannot bear to entertain and confront. It has resulted in great suffering which has created the disease, premature death, and the inhumanity of person to person, group to group, through generations.

The suppression of subconscious thoughts is becoming more and more difficult as the pressure to become totally conscious, real, and authentic is mounting in these times. Ultimately it means that every single person on this planet will have no choice but to be true to themselves if they are to remain here and participate in the New Earth. All the subconscious thoughts of all humans, what has been called 'negative karma', has risen. It cannot be hidden. You see it in your sensing of how the people you meet seem to be more transparent. Their hidden agendas are no longer hidden. They are all coming to the surface. You see it in public figures whose various lies are being exposed. Our governments, corporations, education, medical, and religious institutions are no longer able to hide their intentions. These systems are breaking down and will continue to do so as long as they are based on lies, deception, and half truths. The truth is being revealed and it will continue to undermine the lies at an accelerating rate. The truth, while painful will set us free.

So for you, the shadow history, we referred to in the previous chapter, will show itself frequently through your life as you enact and live the various dramas you have chosen. It is all about exposing the archetypal games you have played with yourself and to begin to say "No more". To begin to experience them and to make the decision not to take them seriously. To see them as a reflection of the belief systems you have carried and the judgements you have made about others and yourself. You are becoming totally conscious, for this is the choice of the path to who you really are. Everything you have hidden you must now acknowledge, no matter how minute. Each seed of fear, doubt, guilt, unlovedness, judgement, and unkindness has to be exposed and owned for you to know the fullness of yourself. True compassion will then be part of you for you will be able to understand and know the suffering of all beings anywhere.

## Your Emotional Guidance System

So how do you clear all the unconscious aspects of yourself? How do you free yourself from the control dramas of your life, and the shadowy side of your human nature? How will you know what to do and whether you have done it? A simple answer would be to begin to really trust your feelings and emotions.

As soon as you chose to search for something deeper and more lasting in yourself you set in motion the unfolding of yourself. Your soul fragments started to piece themselves together like a regathering of old friends. If you have consciously chosen the path to regain the fullness of yourself then all is set in motion. There is no special 'spiritual path'. Your life is your path and your emotions and truth feelings are the key to your movement along it.

Your emotions are in fact your energy in motion (e-motion). They give you direct and clear indications of how your energy is blocked or free and how it needs to be expressed. They indicate the truth of the energy flow in you and are your direct road to freedom of self-expression. Emotions have been much maligned. They have been judged as untrustworthy, threatening and dangerous. To express your feeling is to be selfish, antisocial, and egocentric and unreliable. But what we are saying here is that, unless you befriend your emotions and feelings and see them as the teachers of the truth of where you are in any given moment, you will not free your energy from the old belief systems and thoughts that are holding you back.

You are clearing the old patterns and in the natural unfolding of your Self, life circumstances will come to you that will unlock emotions that you may feel you never had. As you expand in your awareness, thoughts will come into your mind and emotions will arise that you appear to have no control of. Thoughts will release emotions and emotions will release thoughts. They will arise in a natural way triggered by events of the day, or dreams, or even appear to arise spontaneously from nowhere ("Where did that thought come from?"). Your emotions are an essential component of your inner guidance system. They are the freeing of energy; anger from blocked self-expression of the past, fear from lack of knowledge of your own power, guilt from remembering yourself as unkind and unforgiving, sadness from separation, joy from connection and expansion, love from being and knowing the truth of you, etc. To befriend and learn from your emotions, without identifying with the drama of whatever event triggered it, is a great step forward in the direction of freedom and opening to self. Emotions in themselves are not negative. What you learn to do is to express their energy in a manner that is constructive to you and does not harm anyone else. After all it is just your energy requiring of you its release to increase the expression of the flow of love and life from within you.

It is often difficult in handling your emotions when a shadow memory arises. We have great difficulty in admitting to the games we play and even more to any seeds of unfeelingness, cruelty, control, distrust, etc. You would prefer to think the best of your intentions even though privately you often suspect the worst. To admit out loud that you have unkind and judgemental thoughts is not easy. But to be honest with self is to be totally honest about inner feeling and to want to examine these without judgement or denial. Everything becomes fair game when it comes to the truth of yourself. Through the promptings from your emotions and feelings you are bringing light to bear on the thoughts and the old belief systems. They will arise naturally and it requires no special effort on your conscious part to set them in motion. As we have said, your intention to know yourself has set your whole unfolding in motion. You are peeling away the untruth, layer by layer. You are learning to not get involved in the drama of the events, and that the emotions generated by such dramas are life mirroring back to you places in you where you have hidden your light in a shadowy myth of the lie that you are not love incarnate.

Be guided by your feeling and emotions. Trust in their direction for it is the authentic you and you cannot go wrong if you follow it. Take the highest point of view with yourself and choose the highest interpretation for any given situation and when the emotion has subsided, run its course, or has been expressed fully, say thankyou. "Thankyou emotional body for your guidance, and thankyou for the lesson learned". "I intend to accept your guidance and learn more of my power from you."

# Conclusion

Now we have outlined a simplified description of our thoughts and emotions, and how they keep us from knowing ourselves. The rest of the book will be about developing a view that will lift you out of past conditioning and into the mainstream of the New Reality, the fifth dimension. It will be about getting to the centre of you and being in a place where you feel more at home, more grounded, more present, more loving, more joyful and more empowered. We will speak of a way of viewing that will take you much further. Much will resonate with you and be familiar but you must use your own discernment. Take what is of value and put aside what does not strike a cord. It is all about your Truth, your path, your liberation, it is not about what I, the author think. There is no right or wrong in any of this. What you choose, what works for you, what takes you further into your joy is what this book is about. We are here to experience and have fun in learning from it. Enlightenment is all about lightening up.

# Chapter 6

# Four Pillars of Enlightenment

## The Age of Enlightenment

We have entered the age of Enlightenment, or the Age of E. The age in which the infusion of new Energies are Enlivening us all. An age whereby humanity, you, become Empowered by consciously Embracing all that you can be through the choices you make every day towards what really Excites and Enthuses you.

In a very real sense we are entering a full blown time and space in which enlightenment will be the state consciousness for all. Enlightenment is not a state of being to be reached as a goal. It is the claiming back of who and what you already are, and have lost touch with during your recent journey in the third density. To enlighten is to illuminate. It is to bring light to bear on yourself and your experiences. You do not have to bring the energy to you. It is already coming increasingly as the photon energetic frequencies are affecting you and the whole of your reality. Your task is to consciously incorporate the energy of light, the frequency of you, into the life choices you make. Into your mind through the choice of what thoughts you want to reside there. Into your emotions by what feelings you choose to nurture. Into your body, by your choices of how to increase its vitality, balance and ease.

Now I have said previously that to become enlightened is to lighten up and to move in this direction we need to get out of our own way. These were not just clever remarks. Our brief analysis of the two sides of the brain clearly tells you that your overly active left side has taken you away from your direct source of experiences that comes from what your sense impression collage is constantly providing. Your world is dominated by the thoughts you have about it. You identify with your thoughts. You are what you think. Yet most of the thoughts are coloured by belief systems of judgement of right or wrong, good or bad. They take you from the present and put you into a past/future timeline. Your senses, on the other hand, provide you with information about now and only now. So to get out of your own way is to move to a point of view, a state of consciousness, in which your thoughts are not defining your experience. Such a state is known as mukti (enlightenment). When what is present becomes your primary experience and the thoughts you have about them are defined by the needs (truth) of the moment, then you are in the flow of life. Stepping beyond your thoughts is the key because once you begin to do this you begin to see that you have taken yourself far too seriously. You begin to see that the dramas you get so involved in are only a play that you are enacting, a movie with a plot that is not fixed. A life story that can change in any direction you desire. You write the script so you can change it. All you need to do is to step back a bit and begin to view life from a higher vantage point.

This step is a small step but, as with the first moon walk, 'a giant leap' for your consciousness and you. To look at your life and yourself without judgement, without being coloured by what you have been told, without any evaluation of wrongness and unlovingness, is to step back into YOU as you really are.

So in what follows we will examine four ways to help make this step back and into yourself. They are not the only ways but they cover truths that are working for so many people right now. Basically the idea is to play, and explore. Not to rigidly adopt the ideas and make them into just another routine that has no feeling or does not produce the changes you desire. It is all about you, your joy, your deeper, and more satisfying feelings. Your sense of life, adventure and power. Your loving centre.

The whole thing about the Age of E is that whatever you decide to do as your practices should be without Efforting. Enlightenment, stepping back into yourself, is so simple, yet it appears difficult only because you try so hard. The difference between work and play is in the attitude. Your practices should be Easy to do and Enjoyable. Take from the ideas of others but make sure that if you are prompted to adapt or change what was given, then that is exactly what you do. Following your own nose will bring you the Enjoyment, the joy, and will be the confirmation of the truth of you and the validity of the journey you are making. Keep it simple.

## 1. Being Present (Earth)

### a. The Breath

Whatever you can do to make yourself truly present will set you free. It is the mind and your thoughts that keep you in the past and future. Letting go of the power of the mind is the key in all the techniques that take you further into yourself. Paradoxically the closest, most direct and simple route to enlightenment is through something you do without thinking about all the time, your breath. Breathing practice has formed the mainstay of yogic tradition, the Buddhist and Zen traditions, the marshal art traditions, Chinese Tai Chi methods, and many more. Sages, and masters of wisdom have taught of the power of the breath and how that you are not just taking in oxygen but also the life force of the universe. The developed methods of these traditions have sought to increase the conscious intake of this prana, or life force, whereby its devotees become more empowered through a more profound connection to nature and to the Divine. Breath is a wonderful, simple, available anytime, anywhere, key to your enlightenment, to being fully present.

So let us begin. Before you go any further in your reading stop for a moment and become aware of your breath. For the next minute or two just sit there and watch your breath going in and out. Do not do anything. Don't try to control your breath in any way just watch it going in and out. Notice what happens to it quite naturally. Then read on.

You may notice many things but when you watch, changes do begin to occur. Your inhaled breath quite naturally wants to go deeper, the breath rate starts to slow down, and its quality seems to move to become gentler and stronger. You do not have to do anything. It will happen by itself if you are no longer trying to do anything. The breath knows how and where to go. It only needs your permission, your allowing, your letting go of control.

Have you noticed that when people are gathering their thoughts they stop breathing for a brief moment. When they are fearful or stressed they take a big and sudden breath in and hold it. Can you imagine what this is doing to the availability of life force to the body and to self? The cumulative effect to yourself is catastrophic for you eventually starve yourself of the energy of life totally.

If you spend some minutes each day set aside to watch your breath and do nothing else, many things will happen. First and foremost, it is the easiest way to become totally present. As you practice you will find that you can use the technique anywhere and any time that your mind stuff, or fear (any emotion), get in the way. In order to cope with any event you need to be present. When you are breathing you are moving energy, prana, life force into yourself. You are also creating a space in which you can be more centred with all the competence you possess.

What you will also find is that the more you can allow the natural flow of the breath the deeper it will take you into yourself. Breath is your direct connection to the Infinite. Letting go and becoming the watcher is so important and a great relief. It allows you to have a rest from the internal, and infernal dialogue that your mind engages in. Sometimes it will be more difficult than others to watch your breath because your mind will kick in, to want to think anything rather than let go. Be patient and understanding with yourself and in the time you have set aside keep coming back to the breath no matter what. If you build a regular practice, no matter how long a period you do it, it will become easier.

Later, once you have practiced this a little you will find that in breathing consciously you can direct this life force into healing and creative manifestation.

In every breath you take you are bringing to yourself the life force, the adamantine particles of creative potential and vitality, the energy of the New Reality. Your DNA and each cell of your body is being enlivened. As you are becoming the conscious Master, you are learning to take back and blend all the energies and aspects of yourself. Along with learning about this **breath of life** from watching it, you can begin to expand and direct its energy in motion on whatever and wherever you desire.

You can enhance your practice by taking more conscious breaths during your day. You will notice that proper breath is directed into your belly rather than your upper chest. The first part of the breath is the inhale. Inhale taking it down and drawing in and then the exhale is the letting go, almost like a sigh, and allowing.

The inhale is the work, or more properly the willing part of the breath, it is longer, while the exhale is letting go and is shorter and requires no effort. The exhale is not driven. For most people it is not easy to totally let go on the exhale. Just as in life we find it so hard to let go. It is about Trust. The breath of life is about connecting through to trust. Letting go without pausing in between.

So the secret of breath is to inhale well, to let go totally and the third part is to connect the two. To naturally convert the shallow exhale into a deep inhale and a deep inhale into a free exhale in a seamless way. Connecting the inhale and exhale so that they roll easily together.

The breath mirrors the life of two sides, the in and the out, the back and the forward, the up and the down, the shallow and the deep. As this develops and you get more and more into this consistent breath you become more aware, more conscious and more present. You become more in the here and now rather than in the past or future, the there and the then.

The amazing thing about the breath is that it connects you immediately to your body. No mental thoughts are there and the breath will allow the energy to the cells that are calling for the life force they have been deprived of for so long. In addition, events in your life which may produce fear become just events in which you are breathing and the breath will take you right through them with ease.

As you practice more the breath naturally becomes deeper and as this happens you begin to make a connection with the Creator, the Divine, the Eternal within yourself. Your sense of Oneness with All That Is begins to grow and deepen. Your breath is the gateway between the physical and the non-physical. Proper breathing allows the life force to move fully within you and it must and will deepen your awareness of your connection to everything.

The way you breathe is the way you live. If your breath is deep, full, and connected then your life is deep, full, and connected. If your breath is partial, shallow, tight and constricted, and irregular, then this is what you live with. Once you get your breath moving properly the energy will flow where it needs to go or where you direct it. With each breath you are bringing more energy into the body, into you, and also to the planet herself as well as to all around you. You are enlivening your reality.

Try not to mix the watching of the breath time with the conscious movement of breath. Keep these practices separate. The former is for the letting go and learning to be fully present, it is for 'passive' self-realisation. The latter is for the active, directed, intentional, growth and creative expression. Two sides of the same place.

With the development of the proper breath you begin to step out of the rational mind and into your higher universal mind which includes making the step to the right we talked about. This natural breath is aligning you to creation, to the primordial vibration of Creation, and at the same time enlivening your awareness of the truth of who you are. You begin to find your own true voice, your sense of knowing and direction to make more empowered choices in your life. You will become more of who you are.

### b. Awareness

Simply being present is to consciously choose to allow whatever is in front of you, what you are experiencing, whatever activity you are engaged in, to be your all for that time. It is the act of being aware, awake and gently focussed. It is without the intensity of concentration. Without motivation to accomplish anything in particular, but to be totally aware of whatever you are experiencing. It is an act of trust. Trust in yourself, your experience and its place in the plan of your own unfolding. Trust in Creation and the universe. Trust in your own process.

To become more aware, more present, all you need to do is become a watcher of your own experience. It is not at all difficult to do this. At a party, gathering, at home with your children, or in your work you will have often caught yourself playing a role. It is like seeing yourself be the mother/father, hostess/host, sister/brother, boss/worker, etc, and acting out the position yet at the same time watching yourself do it. The watcher is just there not judging or evaluating what you are doing, curious and sometimes amused but never judging. This is the understanding and accepting You who resides there within you always. This is the 'watcher' you. You, as the watcher, are always present, it is just that you are unpracticed at taking that point of view. You have allowed the internal dialogue you to dominate your awareness so that the sensing feeling present you has had to take a back seat.

Being present is bringing the watcher back more fully into your conscious awareness, your daily experiencing of yourself. This simple state of awareness in the moment has been called "mindfulness". You become mindful of what is in front of you, what you are doing, what your senses are saying to you, what your body feels, and what your heart tells you. You become awake to all the possibilities around you as they appear and not with any colouring of the mind and its memories, hopes and fears.

This simple awareness takes practice. You have to choose to become more a watcher than a thinker, to be a receptive, non-judgemental vessel, rather than a control freak, motivated by the fear of what has happened and what might happen. As a watcher there is nothing in particular that needs to be done. Your responsibility is to be open to whatever the universe brings to you in the moment and this responsibility has no load with it. It is easy and effortless. All it requires is your attention and trust. Your responsibility is simply your ability to respond fully to that moment by being present.

Apart from making a conscious choice to become more aware, the only other thing you need is practice. At first it is well to develop a little routine that will remind you to choose to be more mindful in what you are doing. Again keep it simple. You will immediately gain benefits. There is no reason why you cannot become the watcher of experience anywhere and any time. The more often you do it the easier it becomes.

Some suggestions:

i) When you are walking anywhere be present by saying to yourself "I listen and I see". Then just be present with what you see and hear around you. Every time your mind starts to classify, organise and describe your experience repeat these words of focus.

ii) When you sit down to eat make a conscious choice to be there with your experience. Really smell the food and taste each mouthful, chewing it deliberately and sensing it when you swallow it. Feel the sensations in your stomach. Try to be present for the whole meal. A curious thing happens with this exercise. You will find that you will not need to eat as much. Mindful eating is both more satisfying and more health filled.

iii) Use a daily routine, like doing the dishes, and make a point of being present. Become aware of the sensations and movements of your body. Continue to bring yourself back to the watcher whenever you notice you get distracted by other thoughts.

iv) Probably the easiest way to become present focussed is to watch your body sensations. We have already discussed the breath but this applies to body experience as well. Become aware of your bodily sensations. When lying in bed at night or taking time to relax, take an inventory of your body. Starting at the feet and see if you can become aware of the presence of each part without moving them. You will at first notice how little you have been aware of what is there but as the watcher in you is given a chance you will find that there is much more experience available to you than you have allowed yourself. With practice you will become aware at a far deeper level of what is going on in you. All you need to do is to make the choice and watch, to be with your body. Is it not an act of love to be present and non judgmental?

v) Deliberately do something you normally do in a different way. For example, if you are right handed write your notes or doodle, or eat your food with the left. Take an alternative route to work or to shops. Because our dominant sense is our sight I used to spend the odd weekend morning with my eyes totally shut. I became blind and had to feel and hear my way around. This was a bit extreme, and at times quite painful, but it made me fully present. The point is that by changing your experiencing of yourself you bring yourself back to the moment. The bonus of doing this is that it actually helps in the rewiring process that is occurring in all of us at this time. In choosing to do things differently you will be breaking old patterns as well as affirming change in your entire awareness.

Finally there are endless opportunities in your daily life to become the watcher and with practice even in your work you will be able to experience all that is necessary to play your full part but without getting caught up in the role you are playing and the dramas being played out by those still choosing the fullness of their 3$^{rd}$ dimensional reality.

I am reminded of a beautiful passage in the Bhagavad Gita (one of the Indian Vedic texts) where the Lord Krishna says to his prince disciple Arjuna "Do your duty, to the best of your ability, without thought of reward, and it will be well for thee".

## 2. The Benevolent Universe (Air)

We are now at a time when all the thoughts of the negation of creation, and the living of the lie that we are not creators is being dissolved at a rapid rate. You are an expression of the Law of Love in action and that is what you are coming to know as you begin to take into your conscious awareness, the Light of the Great Central Sun that is permeating every cell of your body and every aspect of the field and flow that you are.

There need be no more karma if you so choose. Most people think of the Law of Karma as a law of retribution. "As ye sow so shall ye reap", do something bad and something bad will come back to you, do something good and good will return to you. This is not the original meaning of the law. The of Law of Karma originally referred to the fact that as a conscious human being there is no way you can act and not effect others, the world, and in effect the universe. Every act has potential effects on all others and so you constantly impart movement to the wheel of life and the consciousness reservoir of All That Is. The Law of Karma is the Law of Action not attraction. Karma is the call of the universe to action. Your Karma is the acts you are asked to engage in by the Universe as it brings to you the opportunities to express yourself and be yourself based on the call from within you of what you are and how you see yourself.

So when I say that there is no more Karma what I am really referring to is the belief that there is a universal law of retribution. That people must pay for their deeds and that happiness comes to people who do good things. This has not been reality for so many people. Our sense of justice and fair play is not born out by what has actually happened. You can easily identify with a victim of a rape but can you identify with the perpetrator. If the person has paid for their crime it is easier but forgiveness without paying a debt is extremely difficult to accept. A Law of payback makes it far easier for you to live with acts of violence.

What I am saying is that the principle of retribution is outmoded and is totally at variance with the Law of Love. It was a law created in the minds of humankind to make more sense of the fact that our life often seems so cruel and unfair. Now all the patterns of thoughts and behaviour in the human consciousness that have initiated and perpetuated the lie that we are not creators of our own reality, are coming to the surface. Every single person on this planet is playing out some aspect or remnant of the beliefs of retribution for it to be cleared once and for all. It is not a debt being honoured but an act of alchemy whereby all is being brought into our light and sight and we are in turn dissolving it into the nothingness from which it came through our loving understanding and forgiveness. There will be no more if you say so.

The Universe is totally benevolent. The law we have been seeing as the Law of Karma is really the Law of Manifestation. As you think so it becomes because you are and always have been a creator. What you believe becomes what you experience. The Universe knows only one thing with regards to you and that is, to give you what you desire, what you believe is possible, and what confirms how you experience yourself. The universe can only say "Yes" to you no matter what you ask for, what you mirror or project. One way or another the universe will provide you with the experiences that confirm your view of yourself, your alignment with your reality, whatever you identify with.

I am reminded of the story of Aladdin. The lamp that he rubbed represents your light and your truth and the magnificent genie that grants every wish is the Universe granting all that your thoughts and beliefs are projecting. The Universe while being totally benevolent can see right through and into you however, and will grant whatever you need according to your greatest eternal good and does not bring anything that does not serve your highest purpose. How loving is that?

So you do not have to worry about getting what you need the Universe is the "Bestower" and all you require in abundance will come. Your greatest good is already assured, it is just that you don't fully believe in it yet.

The Universe, which includes you as an essential, vital and eternal part, is unfolding perfectly just as it should and everything is in its place. Everything is where and when it should be. Nothing is out of place or time, and all is complete. To be able to accept this is a huge step towards enlightenment. To practice the attitude and a sense of complete trust, that you do not have to work out all of the whys and wherefores of life to be happy. If you believe in the benevolence of the Universe, that it will bring whatever you need at the right time in the right place, then you can relax and live more in the present.

To begin to really let go we are saying here that you must begin to trust in Creation. To consciously relax at the wheel and let the Universe show you the direction to go by providing you with the opportunities and situations to make the changes necessary to be a fuller expression of yourself and your own joy.

A practice I have found very helpful for many people is to consciously affirm the letting go to the Universe, (God, Tao, or whatever you use to picture that Greater reality which you are a part of) when you sit down to meditate, or at the beginning of the day with intention before you get up.

When you sit down to be in your quiet space say to yourself something like this. "The Universe is unfolding perfectly as it should. For at least this time I will watch and allow this to be. There is nothing special to be or do because all is in its place". Keep it simple but not ritualistic. Say it mindfully. Let it sink in and relax. With practice it can become a part of your understanding, a part of your knowing, a part of your reminders of the centre of who you are.

As you begin to trust in the benevolence of the Universe and stop trying to preconceive everything you will begin to truly understand that there is no such thing as an accident or luck. You will see more and more events coming together in a wonderful synchrony. You get out of your own way so that you see things happen in apparently miraculous ways and with perfect timing. You are allowing the flow of life and at the same time seeing events differently. Viewing it as a beautiful dance of the unfolding of life, all around and within you. All that is required is that you invite and allow the benevolence of the universe into your life. As you look and watch for it, rather than try to reach out and grab it, or will it, then you will begin to see the benevolence work for you and for everyone around you.

## 3. Listening and Trust (Water)

We have spoken of Karma and the pressure to act on and in your reality. It is the call of the outer and there is a corresponding call within you. This is referred to in the Indian Vedic teachings as 'dharma'. Dharma is often equated with the idea of doing ones duty as if it were somehow imposed from some Divine authority but actually it refers to the law of your own unfolding. Just as the Universe unfolds and evolves so do you. You have a blueprint which is unique to you and it lays down possibilities and sequences that make possible the highest expression of you in any given moment. Dharma is thus a pressure within you to be who you really are and it provides exact steps for you to follow to be the best expression of that. Thus to do your Duty is to follow your inner guidance system to the best of your ability and knowing. The Plan for the perfection of you, Your Plan, is already there within you in all its potential. Your job is to follow the steps but to do this requires that you develop trust in the whole process and direction of your own unfolding. To do this you have to be able to listen and listen well.

Your trust in your own process can only come about when you learn to listen to what is going on inside, to act on the directions given, and then discover through the experiences that you are always right with regards to knowing your greatest good.

Everyone has an inner voice and everyone has heard this voice all their life no matter how faint. You learn to shut it off, ignore or deny it but it resurfaces constantly. When you have been led to believe that as humans, you cannot trust your inner nature, that your imagination is out of touch with what is real, that if you experience something that others do not recognise that you are a danger to others and yourself, that power, and love must be obtained from things outside of you and not in your own control, is it any wonder that you learn to doubt that faint voice within.

The New Reality will not allow you to do this any more. It is becoming stronger in everyone. The more chaotic the world of human affairs becomes, the stronger the voice for change in you is becoming. You cannot ignore it for much longer. There is no choice now but to hear it and it will not go away. However, have you not noticed that when you listen to this voice when you trust and take the courage to respond to its direction it is always right? It leads to unexpected and often great possibilities and experiences in your life. The more you trust in this voice the more you learn and the more beneficial the outcomes.

Being able to listen and being open to oneself and trusting in the process of unfolding, without interference, is a mark of enlightenment. To hear one's Higher Self, to be open to knowledge and direction without having to know exact outcomes. To have the courage to trust completely oneself without having an inkling of where it is leading. This is a mark of enlightenment. It is time for you to take a clearer, more intended and conscious route to your inner guidance system.

In order to improve your relationship to your intuitive inner voice, your Higher Self, to be in synchronisation with your dharma, it is necessary to develop an attitude of active listening. To consciously tell yourself that you are willing to be open and listen to your own guidance. Suspending your own normal frame of reference is important in order to fully attend to the voice and feelings within. To frequently stop in your day and to tune into yourself even if there is nothing in particular that arises. To make a point of acting on your prompting, even though you may not easily understand why you need to do what you are prompted to do, or what the result will be. Sometimes the action is for you but sometimes you will do something that is very important for someone else acting in a totally different drama. Understanding everything is not the point but trusting is, and you will find that you will always be guided to do the right thing by yourself and by others. It is not about learning to be an obedient servant. It is about learning to trust your inner guidance which is part of you and which knows all that is necessary in any given moment. The depth and truth of you in total harmony with the Plan, Your Plan, the law of your own ascension.

In being willing to listen, to allow, and to follow your own inner guidance you are taking a precise and fool proof journey that guarantees your success. The blueprint to your truth is waiting for you. It is directed by your Being and only requires your conscious intention to listen and to act on that direction. All is then set in motion.

Your truth, your path is there in the language of your heart, in the messages from your body, in the warm and gentle words of your guides and helpers who know you so well and are in complete resonance with who you are. All can be felt, spoken to and will speak to you. Believe it and use it.

There will be times when you are asked to do things that seem out of context with whatever you are doing in the moment, and yet in responding you are in training. You are training yourself to listen out of the blue, to be awake to your promptings anytime, anywhere. For example, I remember driving along a highway and suddenly feeling a prompt to pull over by a small group of shops. I did so and ended in a small second hand store where, in a prominent place was an almost new pair of smart looking shoes that fitted me perfectly. I bought the shoes and went on my way. The buying of the shoes was not vital to my future nor appeared to be linked to anything very important, though I now had lovely pair of very cheap shoes. The event was, however, another confirmation for me of how my listening and response leads to a synchronous and benevolent flow. It will be part of your training to experience the little miracles of your own truth feelings. Gradually it will become part of the way you live, miraculously.

Many opportunities will present themselves. You will be asked often and increasingly to be of service to others by taking your courage to respond in situations where you will doubt yourself or have feelings of self-consciousness. Most of these events will be everyday situations in which, for example, you may feel prompted to go and talk to a stranger you see out of the corner of your eye, and it turns out to be very helpful to the other. Much of the love you have to give others is held back because you are self-conscious, embarrassed, and doubt the efficacy of your own inner guides. Only experience will prove otherwise. In responding to your inner voice you are in training to be the touch of love.

To move beyond the belief that you are making things up in your own mind is a big step. The practice of allowing the impressions, feelings, and thoughts to arise is absolutely essential if you are to discover what you really are and the fountain of knowledge and understanding you have access to in your Being.

Active and open listening can be directed toward any question, decision, opinion you have about anything. As with trusting the truth of what others say, learning to trust yourself requires you to use your discernment. Learning to test, from your own experience, whether something works for you. You are learning to become more empowered in your life by accessing that which enriches you by helping you to make more appropriate choices in your life.

The laws of the unfolding of the Universe and the unfolding of You are in absolute harmony. It is a most perfected dance. So why not try more. And if you already do listen from time to time, do it more in your life and watch the miracles happen.

## 4. Holy Presence (Fire)

We have talked about being in the present. When you are in the present you are in the experience of your own presence. You are you without any future projection or past memory. You are in the experience of yourself. You are naturally centred because your presence can be nothing else than balanced and at home. You are in your natural unencumbered self experience. Everything just Is. You are not seeing, thinking or doing you just are. There is a profound stillness, a peace and a smooth flow of connection to all that is there in your presence. A Oneness, like an ocean of experience with no separations between yourself and what you are experiencing.

It is here in your Presence that you begin to know the enormity of who you are. It is here that you feel the flow of your love for all creation because the feeling of connection and Oneness becomes undeniable. Your Presence is the Divine Presence which pervades all and is All.

The experience of Presence comes not from seeking to attain it. It comes from the willingness to let go of all that which you cling to as being necessary for who you think you are in the world. You cannot be in your Presence and be conscious of a separate "I". Remember we said that you are what you identify with. So part of the trick is to begin to identify with that within you that you cannot put limits on but that stands for the highest expression of you.

You are love incarnate. You have been fashioned by a limitless ineffable Love Consciousness. You are Divine Love in expression in this reality and you could be nothing else, however you experience yourself at this time. Your Presence is the Presence of the Divine and if you would know God then you must learn to sit in your own Presence.

I am reminded of a time when I went to visit a holy man in India many years ago. Much had been said about this man, his powers and miracles, and I wanted to see for myself with the faint hope of something profound happening to me

80

being in his presence. It was early morning when I arrived at the ashram and I joined the many hundreds of devotees sitting quietly waiting for their beloved guru to arrive and give them his blessing. As I sat there I became aware of a great stillness and sense of peace not only filling me but also in the very air around the whole gathering. A feeling of great love filled me and pervaded the whole compound where we all sat. It was as though it could be touched it was so strong. We all waited for over an hour before the guru arrived. I expected his love to add to that which was all around but this did not happen. The Peace and the Love remained but I realised that it was not the guru's Presence I was feeling but the Presence of the devotees sitting in their truth. Watching and waiting in their own peace and love. And that the Presence I was feeling within myself was my own Presence initiated by the devotees sitting in their own Presence. What a wonderful lesson for me to learn, that what I sought could be enlivened by being in the Presence of others but that the Presence I feel can only be my own.

Whenever you feel that stillness you are in the Holy Presence. Whether it is with a Master, a great teacher, a mother loving her child, a baby smiling, under a tree in the forest, the Presence you feel in the Love, in the Peace or simply in the stillness, you are in the presence of the most Holy Self which you are.

How profound and magnificent you are. This, in my opinion, is singly the most compelling reason to practice meditation. To be able to experience the profound stillness that brings you so close to your Greater Divine Self and to the feeling of growing, blending and melding together is beyond words to describe.

It is easy to see now why it becomes imperative for you to drop all beliefs that you are unlovable, and unworthy, and take up in its fullest the knowing of your magnificent origin, the fact that love has always been and always will be your nature. It has been so difficult for humans to forgive themselves and cast aside the messages of hate and distrust.

It is now time to do so. To stop "pussyfooting" around, to stand tall and take ownership for what you are rather than being afraid for what you might have been. Why is it so difficult to invite the Higher Self of what you are to dine at your table as a mentor and friend? The more you identify with the highest of yourself, love yourself and befriend all that you are, the easier experiencing your Presence, your Love becomes.

You know this Presence for you have sensed it in others. People walk into a room, into a shop and you can feel something strong, still and radiant coming from them. Anyone who has attended a meditation circle will have experienced the peace and stillness immediately following, that is not just within themselves but that is in the room.

Being more present is walking in Grace, where every step becomes a blessing to this world, not because you consciously direct it all the time, but because you are inviting Presence. Your Presence is palpable even to those who are as yet asleep to themselves.

# Chapter 7

# Field and Form

In this chapter we will outline a view of the energy system that you are in order to get a sense of the wonder and potential of the expression of you. It will be kept simple. There are many good sources of knowledge and practical guides elsewhere for an in depth study of any one of the ideas we will cover here. In these times new methods of energy and quantum healing are beginning to flourish which can greatly assist you along your self-discovery path if you so desire. My objective here is to deepen your sense of awe, power and ownership of the energy that you are. Getting a better understanding of your boundaries will help the integration of the new energies into your conscious awareness and increase the ease with which transitions can be made into your expansion. If you expand your love and consciously draw in the light of creation then you do not have to know anything in particular for it to work. However, consciously developing your knowledge is a part of self-mastery and, at the very least, changes your sense of who you are, your identity, and your power to affect the changes you desire in yourself.

Remember that you came here from a place far within and beyond the self that you currently experience. You came to experience many things and it is now time to gather up the fragments you have left scattered in many places and many dimensions. It is time for the ego ( your free will love based choices) to play its proper part in the service of your soul, through your directed intention, and for your soul to merge more fully with your Higher Self, your Godhead and the Source of All That Is. It is time to rediscover your true nature as an energetic Being while the energy changes within you unfold the plan and dynamics of your ascension.

The total field of you is an elaborate energy system in constant movement. It is a field of interweaving, interpenetrating waves of energy frequencies. There are energy vortices (like reception and transmission stations) that move the different frequency waves through the system and between the layers of energy. There are meridians (like channels and pipelines) that allow the energies to move to specific points in the system. Each sub-system is intimately connected to all others by light strings and is patterned with an elaborate gridwork that makes up the blueprint for your energy system.

Your energetic field is also an information highway. It collects, stores and distributes information for the movement of energy in any part of the system. From the New Reality perspective, your energetic system has available to it, through the DNA all the potential and information for the entire evolution of life on earth, not to mention human evolution, your ancestors physical and experiential records, your own past lives and all of your current life. The information is there in your field as a potential to be read off and activated in and through your physical, mental and emotional experience.

## Your Energetic Environment

What follows are some of the divisions commonly used to outline the energy system of you.

To allow the body to be sustained by light you utilize photon energy by tapping into and absorbing the Universal Life Force or 'chi' energy directly into your cells. This occurs through your higher mind mastery where your command and expectation uses the Universal Law of Resonance, where like attracts like. Because you expect the pranic forces to nourish and sustain you, it does. The ability to be sustained by chi or prana is a natural consequence of being in tune with the world you live in. You exist within physical reality in a basic four body system - the physical, emotional, mental and spiritual bodies. When they are out of tune or in imbalance, you experience various degrees of physical, emotional or mental illness or dissatisfaction with life. When they are in tune life becomes exciting and magical.

When these lower bodies (termed lower due to their slower rate of vibration) are tuned to the frequency of the higher bodies then human beings can really live life to their highest potential. If you can tune your bodies and realign your frequencies (the energy signals you transmit and receive) to a purer, more harmonious pitch, you will be able to control the quality and direction of your life and your experience to your own complete enjoyment and satisfaction.

## 1. The Subtle Energy Systems in the Body

The human aura is an electromagnetic field that surrounds the physical body. It is divided into five layers and normally extends two to three feet out from the body. Usually the number of layers is given as seven but for our purposes I have combined the three higher levels into one body which is termed the "light body.

### a. Physical Body

The physical body functions through various systems like the circulatory system, respiratory system, digestive system, etc. From one perspective, the physical body is an extraordinarily complex energy system. It is much more than the biochemical machine the medical model allows for. The energy field that makes up the form of the physical body is the expression of all the higher levels of consciousness manifest within the densest physical plane of existence. The physical body itself has its own consciousness, distinct from the mind and emotions. This is the consciousness of the body as a whole. Moreover, each organ in the body also has its own consciousness, and each tissue in each organ, each cell in each tissue, and so on. In the physical body, as everywhere else, there are varying degrees of consciousness. Although these are usually beneath the level of the normal waking consciousness, through mastery, love, and intent, you have the power to affect any and every cell of your body. You can go right down into the consciousness of the cells and the atoms. This is the consciousness of inanimate matter itself. On a level closer to our ordinary experience, there is the biological physical consciousness of the physical body, the automatic organic functioning and reflexes of the body. Left to itself, the body follows its own instinctual wisdom, transmitted from the spiritual physical consciousness level. All disease and even injury is the result of imprints of negative emotions and belief systems mirrored in the body.

**b.  Emotional Body**

The Emotional Body is the locus of your emotional being, of feelings and emotions, physical likes and dislikes, sensual enjoyment, and aesthetic appreciation. In popular speech, the gross emotional body is referred to as "the gut" while the higher deeper feelings are referred to as "the heart", as opposed to the gross mental body or "the head". This is pointing to the predominant location of the different energy centers where you experience your emotion and feelings.

The emotional body holds deep subconscious patterns of emotions. Restrictions here will usually come from early imprinting in your childhood from your immediate family (parents, grandparents, siblings) or early caregivers from the time of conception to about age seven. These are subconscious restrictions which rarely can be consciously remembered, as they bypassed the conscious mind when they first occurred. Also your ancestral imprinting, passed down from many generations through the emotional subconscious is held and expressed through your emotional body as are your belief systems. Restrictions from beliefs and mental constructs that we formulate in order to cope with different stressful situations in life, particularly during our formative years, result in emotional problems that arise later in life, long after the original stressful stimulus is gone. As you are currently experiencing, often your thinking and beliefs are still subtly organized in such a way that they no longer serve the best interests of how you presently see yourself and your potential.

### c. The Mental Body

There are two levels of Mental Body, there is the more concrete mental thinking and a higher or abstract mental, which somewhat corresponds to the two sides of the brain functioning that were described earlier. The mental body facilitates cognition, the faculty of knowing and the filter of your language. It gives you the ability to discern, and to have thoughts, beliefs, concepts, and higher psychic abilities. Mental consciousness ranges from discernment of the very specific, detailed, and particular, to the discernment of the very general, inclusive, and abstract. Differentiating, distinguishing thought to inclusive, embracing thought.

The mental body has its own range of feeling. When there is excessive focus within the limiting, analytical range of thought then there is judgment, mental fear, and depression. When thought expands into the more unifying scope then there is compassionate understanding, peace, joy, awe, and bliss.

Thoughts build actual forms in the ether which we project out from our mental body and can, not only be seen as quite distinct by those with "sight", but also can be sensed by others from the continuous waves they give off. Your mind is the window through which you look at the world around you. It needs to be clear as crystal if it is to pour forth your Presence to the world. You can only receive thoughts of perfection from your Diamond Self if your mental body is cleared of thought forms of imperfection. Imperfections are simply held untruths of who and what you are in essence.

### d. Etheric Body

The Etheric Body is the subtle life-force body, which sustains the life of the physical body, and serves as the mould or matrix for physical metabolic functions. The etheric body gives vitality, health, life and organization to the physical body. It attunes your consciousness to the principles of Energy. It steps energies from the higher bodies down into our physical consciousness. The etheric body is the subtle level of the physical body. It is composed of various energies such as electromagnetic, chi, vitality, etc. The etheric body has a figure form in the same shape as the physical body. This figure form is made of numerous energy channels called nadis or meridians and of course the chakra system. This is what you would call a body template and translates how the energies of the mental, emotional, and higher bodies will be expressed in the physical. Any change in the etheric body will be registered on and in the physical body.

### e. Light Body

The Light Body contains all consciousness and virtues cultivated in each of your lifetimes, especially that developed will power, love, wisdom, and creative intelligence. It is built out of all the knowledge gained from of all past lives, and experience far beyond. It is the treasure chest that keeps eternally safe all the fruits of all your past experiences. It is the vehicle that facilitates the unfolding of consciousness that you use physically, emotionally, mentally, and spiritually. It is the vehicle for human immortality, whether you are in incarnation or not. The light body is the central focal point of consciousness itself for the entire human being. Therefore, its range of consciousness includes the physical, etheric, emotional, and mental. Your Soul's life, you, is one of unity, group consciousness, love, wisdom, bliss, and purpose. As you spiritually awaken you extend its range of consciousness into the Higher Mind feeling and awareness and become constantly conscious of your Oneness with the Source of All That Is.

Viewed from a three dimensional perspective your light body appears as a radiant orb of white and golden light, a miniature sun, approximately 30 feet in diameter. It has vortices on the top and bottom, lines of light and sparkling and radiant energy throughout.

## 2. Vital Energy

### a. Life Force

The composition of your bodies is of ethers, atoms and cells which hold energy and information. God, the Creative Loving Consciousness and potential is everywhere and is a pure intelligent energy field that sustains all life. You can go within yourself, contact and direct this energy of your own God Self. The more you identify with your source the more you can utilize and direct your life force. And by the law of attraction the more you identify with your source the more the energy of Creation flows through you and activates the information and energy release that leads to the fullest unfoldment of you as you really are.

The vital energy comes to your physical form from two directions and one basic source. First radiating from the Great Central Sun through our Sun and down through a vortex just above your head through your entire body. The second route moves through the centre of the Earth and up through your body through a vortex just below the base of your spine and also through your feet. This two way flow is the Alpha and Omega of your being here now.

### b. Kundalini

The second vital energy in the body is known as Kundalini. This spiritual energy is present within everyone from birth; it is not acquired from any external source. This energy lies in an unmanifest, potential state as a sleeping spiritual energy centre at the base of your spine. This dormant energy becomes transformed and is activated through your will, desire and love and is known as transformed energy (like kinetic energy). As the Kundalini is activated it gradually burns off the excesses of a person's desires, conscious addictions, sub-conscious mind and ego and facilitates the merging back of the individual with their Source, God. In these times this energy becomes naturally activated as you transmute the experiences of the past into knowledge of understanding and compassion.

## 3. Chakra Centres

Just as the heart is the principle centre (organ) of the circulatory system and the brain of the nervous system, similarly the subtle energy system has various centers or chakras. Chakra is a Sanskrit word meaning "wheel". There are seven major chakras and many minor chakras in the human energy system. They are energy points in the form of a vortex that spin in a clockwise direction at various speeds. They emanate from both the front and back of your body. Chakras send out energy and receive energy and can be open or closed, excessive or deficient, or any of the various stages in between. Ideally the chakras need to be in balance with each other. There should be an even flow of energy through all of the chakras. The motion of the chakras are quite directly and specifically related to the glandular system at the physical level, both our positive and negative feelings at an emotional level, and our conscious and unconscious thought processes at a mental level.

There are seven major chakras for the physical body, though this number is in the process of changing gradually as human consciousness is changing. The new blueprint and DNA has already seeded another six major energy entry points. The seven major chakras are situated just above the crown of the head (Crown chakra), in the middle of the forehead between the eyes (Brow chakra), below the chin on the throat (Throat chakra), in middle of chest just above the heart (Heart chakra), to left of body between heart and navel (Spleen chakra), just below the navel (Navel chakra), and at the base of the spine (Root Chakra). The higher up the body a chakra is located the increasingly more complex they become as they handle greater complexity of integration of energy waves of the life force. You have many other chakra points notably those in the hands and feet, and some extend into the Earth, while others are situated well above the head. Each level of the subtle body system has its own set of chakras and as the layers extend outward the chakras vibrate at higher rates. This way, energy can be transmuted between all bodies through all these energy vortices.

The first three major chakras from the base of the spine upwards you can think of as primarily having to do with your physical survival, while the three upmost have to do with your spiritual and higher consciousness flow of the life force. The Shift that is now upon us is about blending and balancing the energy by becoming centered in your heart, through your conscious intention to live and be guided by your love and your passion. This means to allow the energies coming up in a natural way, from the lower three vortex energy points, to be infused with clarity and expansiveness of the Truth of you, bought to you through the upper chakras, and blending the two in your heart through your own free will with the loving understanding that you are taking ever increasing ownership for all that you are. This is accomplished by centering your consciousness in the location around your heart chakra. Letting this become the primary locus for you and your life experience. Allowing, guiding and intending your awareness there to direct your choices. Letting go of the brain as the locus of your decision making. This is the manner in which you will wake up, this is the way to the complete removal of all your doubt and fear, and this is the way you will receive all the knowledge and wisdom you could ever desire and complete and total healing from any blockage or dis-ease.

## 4. Field matrix - A New Body

Now something very profound is happening to all of humanity. Nothing is fixed in Creation, everything is in a state of change. For any event there is a potential form of multiple outcomes, some outcomes seem more likely than others. It seemed that, coming up towards the year 2000, humanity was on a course of self-destruction, the

Armageddon. The consciousness of humanity appeared to be unable and unwilling to break the cycle of suffering and self punishment. The deep cries of powerlessness and hopelessness seem all pervasive. Humanity and Earth had learned all it could about pain, unlovingness and separateness and it was time to regroup.

As a result of the intent of so many who dreamed of a better world, and who knew and had been holding the remembrance and intent of love to rule human affairs for so many years, something miraculous happened to change the scales of decision for our survival and possibly the survival of the Earth. A critical mass was reached such that the collective unconscious of humanity altered. It made a full 180 degree turn around from hopelessness to hope, from nightmare to vision, from looking back at fear to looking forward into the eyes of love. This is what a million or so 'lightworkers' have held as a vision that has engaged and become firmly embedded in the unconsciousness of all humanity. It is stirring within all but more than that. It has guaranteed the path of the change into the future. The path can be rocky or smooth, it is up to you, but Paradise beyond what we can presently possibly imagine, is assured.

The pattern of change that is occurring within us is being reflected and facilitated by a truly amazing development in our energy field. A gridwork is forming which allows for the direct and instant reading of any and all elements of what we are and have experienced from the subtle bodies we have described.

This gridwork is in the form of a flow that extends about arms length right around the body including 18 inches above the head and below the feet. It consists of strings of golden-white light with little gem like light beads, or light discs, stringed together and moving along pathways up the outside of the field and down through the top of the head, down the spine, out at the base of the spine down to 18" below the feet and back up on the outer edge of your auric field. These light strings surround your body and are all moving in the same direction down through a point (The Alpha point) 18 inches above the crown chakra, through a pillar of light sheathing your spine and out through a point (Omega point) 18 inches below the base of the spine down to a point 18 inches below the feet, and back up the boundary of your field.

The beads of light on the strings hold the information on all that you as a soul have ever experienced. They contain records of your hereditary patterns and the memory and feeling of every experience you came into this life with and all those things you have experienced during this life. This gridwork of light strings also holds all those things you are forming in your future which includes any fear or worry filled events that you tend to create in your life and the hopes and dreams you are consciously intending to manifest. In short your Field Light Matrix holds the information for your entire electromagnetic field just as your two physical DNA strands hold the information for the entire physical evolution of your body, your ancestral history, and the physical characteristics you now possess. The Field Light Matrix holds all the information from your various energy bodies, your crystalline memory structures and your DNA encoding.

The emergence of this patterned structure allows you to have available any and all information necessary for clearing your entire energy system of imbalances and keying into both your potential and the past talents you have acquired but have forgotten.

### a. Informational Light Seeds.

The light beads that line and travel along the light string pathways of your field matrix include the knowledge and memory of all that you are as well as what you have taken on through the life choices you have made. These encodements, that mostly provide the information of how you experience yourself at present, are basically of two kinds. **Natural** encodements which define the nature of your expression. They are the choices of what you wanted to bring with you when you incarnated. These are based on soul choice in harmony with your Being and the heart of the Spirit of the Earth (Gaia) whose field is your immediate environment. While natural encodements provide limits to your expression they are set to be totally in harmony with your soul purpose, the Law of your own Unfolding.

There are also **artificial** encodements which have been imprinted from your experiences and which now provide a dominant and continual influence on how you see and experience yourselves. These encodements are reflected in many of the conscious and unconscious beliefs you hold about yourself and your world. They are in continual movement in your field and as your light quotient is increasing and your field matrix is becoming more activated your artificial encodements will not leave you alone. These artifical encodements are what you are in the process of releasing to allow more of your truth and potential to emerge in your conscious awareness. You have artifical encodements for most things you have experienced. For example, blockages to the expression of your love come from all the beliefs of doubt you hold about unworthiness, lack of power, fear of failure, need to be perfect, etc. These are artificial encodements that prevent and maintain your feelings of unlovedness. The good news is that artificial encodements can be easily released and we will speak more of this later in Chapter 8.

### b. Infinity Pathways

Information from the gridwork light strings feed into your body and awareness through a myriad of pathways. These pathways move in the pattern of infinity, ie the figure of eight (8) and they enter your body and into your spinal light centre through the chakra vortices. They leave at the same point they entered and feed back to your field in a rhythmic dance. As you become more balance in field and form these lighted "eight" pathways become more active and synchronized. Again they are being naturally activated but conscious intent will enhance their development and unfoldment. Infinity loops blend in Oneness the experience of you and the Universe in an eternal cycle.

### c. Crystaline Form.

You are becoming a crystalline being as you blend the 3$^{rd}$ and through the 4$^{th}$ to the 5$^{th}$ vibrational wave of your Being. What does this mean? It does not mean that we are becoming solid, inanimate, and clear like the mineral crystals. We are using "crystal' in the sense of the energy matrix that gives it the perfected form and characteristics that we see in mineral crystals. What is happening is that as your field light grid develops, and becomes more defined and balance and activated by your conscious intent, feelings, thoughts and actions, the lines of force set up a diamond shaped energy dynamic extending inwards from the boundaries of your field to your central spine at the region of your heart centre. The apex points of the diamond are focused 18" above and below your body. The Diamond Self of you. This beautiful perfecting energy crystal replicates itself in smaller versions firstly within your heart as your love grows. There is another developing between your heart and head centre. Interestingly, the major mineral constituent of our bodies is carbon. The perfected carbon which has the power to receive and emit energy and information with clarity is pure diamond. Visualise and meditated on your Diamond Self. It can take you far in your alignment with Self.

### d. Pillar of Light

There is a column of pure light that runs straight down through the centre of the body. It contains the descending and ascending pathways of your life force, as we have described. Also it is your direct and immediately available connection to the Universal Energy Field where the energy strings of your field merge and flow within you. Its centre holds your spiritual intelligence, your keys to self-mastery like absolute love, joy, compassion, balance, wisdom, and discernment. They are present in you always.

Your locus in any awareness exercise will start and end somewhere within this column for in a sense, this is the centre in which you bring the Universe to you and from which you give your essence to the Universe.

What does all this about your field matrix mean? It means that all that was buried in your unconsciousness and super consciousness has now 'surfaced' and is available to be read off, assimilated and owned consciously by you. It does not require the all consuming disciplines of the ascetic mastery that the saints and masters of the past had to engage in. All is available to you. Your quantum field is brimming with unlimited knowledge and potential. It will come to light in anyone in a natural unfolding and personalized sequence and timing of experiences. The speed of your ascent depends on your capacity to hold the light and own your lovingness. It will also depend on the progress of others for we are intimately connected and the ascent of one is the ascent of us all. Your progress into your potential can be enhanced by directed and concentrated intent to gain a more intimate knowledge of your field and engage in exercises that enhance the flow of energy within and about you. For those whose inclination is to further their depth of understanding and practice, there are a number of very powerful and enlightened practices that have recently become available. However, taking any energy movement system and modifying it to your needs will be of great benefit if it is done with conscious intent and lightness of heart.

## A Simple Exercise for Conscious Grid Alignment

a. **Consciously Define Your Field.** Get a feel for your field by stretching your arm out in front of you and drawing an arc as far round as you can. Imagine a circle going on right round behind you. Now imagine the boundaries of you the same distance from your body all the way up and down. See an oval from 18 inches below your feet to 18 inches above your head.

This whole area contains your field. These are your 'boundaries' so that when you feel restricted come back to defining your boundaries and the whole field within and without filled with brilliant golden light.

b. **Consciously Visualize Your Grid.** See a grid of pulsating golden light strings (like a gilded cage) surrounding you within the light. Visualise brilliant light travelling up all around you and arching over and pouring down through the top of your head.

c. **Breath in the Essences of Your Field.** Breath in and down the golden essence from the Alpha point above your head through the top of your head and down to the heart, pause and allow the breath to travel the rest of the way down out the bottom of the spine to the Omega point where it will naturally move around below your feet and back up. Three such conscious breaths are sufficient.

## Where Do You Start

Our beloved Earth Mother, Gaia, is going through a process of realigning herself with the new energies she is being bathed in. In her period of global warming she is burning the old accumulated and denser vibrations and clearing the way for a harmonious blending with her new reality. She is adjusting her energy grid into a new design template.

What seems without is now living within you. Your Kundalini achieves this same effect by slowly and gradually burning off the old belief systems of the past that you are willing to let go of, and clearing the channels for the free movement of the increasing life force within you by moving the freed energy up the spine and out to creation and the old outmoded "illusions' down and out into the centre of the Earth. You have bodies that are directly being crystal wired for Bliss. You have an energy grid already in place and evolving. The two halves of your brain are being rewired so that the veil between is disappearing. You are being showered with the energy of the Great Central Sun and it is building within you and being activated by the extent you are willing to acknowledge and own it.

Your grid, however, has blocks and distortions that affects the energy that flows along it. Your task is to clean up the energy lines. You clean and purify the system through your awareness, by embracing all experiences that are coming to you, and by your willingness to love, and to forgive and let go of your pain, suffering and fear. Your task is to open up to the energy in the Universe. This is done by what you eat, drink and breathe. Not just that, but more importantly, with what attitude and feeling you do them with. How you sit, how you stand, how you move and how you live.

Just recognising that you are a vibrant energy system is a big step in the right direction. It means you need to listen and feel within yourself. What is within is going to touch and teach you if you are willing. When you start feeling you are an internal energy system you can start cooperating with it. After all it is you. There is this Force within you that wants you to evolve. It isn't trying to make the path unnecessarily hard, to arbitrarily throw obstacles in your way. As you start to feel a harmony within you consciously use this Force. It will change anything you wish within you if you intend, ask and trust. Prove this to yourself. Remember in the movie Star Wars, "Use the Force Luke". The force from your intent, to breathe the vital energy, the light, to any part of the energy system that you are. Do it with ease and lovingly.

Chapter 8

# Knowing and Healing

Healing, whether of the body, emotions, mind, or spirit, is about attaining a balance. Attaining a harmony between your mind and your heart. You are the only one who can perform healing that will endure because all disease, blockage, and imbalance in you are held by you in your own unconsciousness. Held by the beliefs you have maintained about your powerlessness and disconnection from the energy of Creation and the reality that you, as a consciousness, can manifest anything because you are existing in a quantum field where the reality is limitless potentiality created through your own intention. The very fact that you are experiencing imbalances is testimony to your own power to create. Disease has nothing to do with your worth. Health is not a result of having been bad or good. It has to do with your Life Force.

So in fact the simple answer to health and wellbeing is to become more conscious of all that you are, for in doing so you will be able to directly choose what you keep in your field and what you no longer require. This leads to a complete and full flow of Life Force, Chi, in your form and field. To become fully conscious is to become totally free to choose, free to be in harmony with yourself and all you experience. Knowledge, of what has been unconscious, is the key to what is holding you back and since, as we have said, all the keys (the appropriate knowledge for you personally) are now available to you in a programmed sequence in your field grid, as well as in a Universe that is poised to grant you your every wish, then what is stopping you from gaining total health?

It is your mind, or what I call the 'mental mind'. That part of your mind that is connected to your memory, that thinks in a timeline (past/present/future), and that maintains and identifies with the view of you and your consciousness of you as separate from the field of you and the field (consciousness) of All That Is.

## Mind and Knowing

### Hidden Mind - Subconscious

The mind can be seen as having three different places and functions. First the contents of the subconscious mind, located in your field, enters at the navel chakra from both the mental and emotional body via the field grid. Now whatever you desire strongly, or think about or imagine, drops into this subconscious region, and is recorded there. The more energy we put into these thoughts and feelings, the more the subconscious energy is attracted to the images. Each and every one of these impressions are then carried out in their minutest detail in your life through subtle and not so subtle thoughts, emotions, dreams, actions and bodily afflictions. Not only have we created subconscious patterns of numerous images and feelings in this lifetime, but within the lower regions of our aura, deeply submerged though they may be, are all the patterns created in past lives. Some of these patterns we have adopted for our present life. They are experienced as pressures in our lives and are set primarily in our childhood as approved or disapprove thoughts, emotions and reaction patterns that continually reoccur. Any thought that has been important to you and you have ignored, avoided, denied, or repressed will be there. Once you bring any subconscious thought into the light of your conscious mind, take ownership for it as having been generated by you, examine the truth of it against the Truth of who you really are, it become conscious experience and moves to be part of your knowing.

# Mental Mind

The locus of feeling, where you generally feel you are coming from as a consciousness, is in your head. This is why it has been so easy to identify the brain as the source of our thinking and knowing and the place of our mind. Purely and simply people believe that what they are is what they think and that if they stopped thinking and trying to be somebody and let go of their mind then they would go crazy or fall into oblivion. You (as ego) are literally afraid of losing control and your very identity if you let go of your mind. Fear creates the false ideas, fear perpetuates the mental mind control, fear, produces the perpetual attempts to try to control Creation through the never ending internal dialogue of thinking of how we want Creation to be and continually reliving how it falls short of what we want.

Thus we would rather build our ideas of truth in this mind than accept that it is impossible to hold the glory of the unseen, unlimited potential of Creation in our mental minds and that to do so, separates us from our connection to Creation and our sense of truly belonging. Thus, though it makes perfect sense to see the natural unfolding of Creation in the life of a tree, for example, very few people believe how it could and should be the same for themselves.

The mind unlike the tree will strive for the light and loose its roots in the earth or anchor itself rigidly on earthly things and ignore the call of the sun. But strength and grace come from accepting your earthly conditions and the light of Creation simultaneously. Strength and grace come from suppleness. The tree would break in the wind if it were not flexible. Yet as long as you act and believe that your mind can contain the fullness of the truth of you then you remain rigid and must eventually snap.

Through the duality of thought your mind creates separation. Every thought you have can either lead towards the light or it multiplies your illusions of truth. Thus if your vision of the world is to change then it is in your thoughts of it that you will find both the stumbling blocks and keys to transformation. Nothing, but nothing can impede your own growth except for your own thoughts.

So many people believe that they cannot help what they think. This is entirely untrue. There is no such thing as an 'idle thought' because the world you see is in your perception, your thought. It is your mind and nobody else's. You and you alone hold the power of your own mind. True you can 'in your own mind' give the power to others but it is still your giving it. If you do not believe that the thoughts you have are your own then you have made yourself powerless in your own mind which is an' illusion for it is your mind, you have total and exclusive access to it. You are not just responsible for what you do, you are responsible for everything you think. Anyway what you do comes from what you think.

What is really important is to realise that your mental mind is not the source of your knowing, for you are much more. Your mind and your intelligence is much more. Your mental mind is only your conscious awareness of your beliefs, images, and impression of yourself and your world.

Each thought is enclosed and linked by an energy of feeling (emotion) and so you cannot think without feeling. Whenever you think even in a logical and analytical manner it is clothed in emotion and feeling. If the feeling of those thoughts seems missing it is only because it has been submerged, through experience into the subconscious mind. It takes a great deal of bodily energy to suppress these thought-feelings. It leads to stress and if prolonged, is the root cause of disease and imbalance. Often the predominance of the logical-analytic mind set devoid of apparent feeling experience leads to the contracting and shrinking of the heart and its tributaries with resultant eventual heart attack and death. Mental mind serves the heart not the other way round.

To break the cycles of the mental mind you have to take ownership for your own mind, learn to see that your disharmony is a separation of who you think you are from your knowing (awareness) of yourself. You need to be able to examine courageously, what thoughts you harbour and raise them up, with understanding and love, after they have been honestly examined. You need to learn that when you have certainty in your mind but it goes against the simple truth of your own feelings, then there is work to be done in clearing a controlling pattern in your mind, and thus in your behaviour.

If you are to free yourself you cannot stop the thoughts that come into your head. You can, however, choose what thoughts remain. Your mental mind provides the conscious working map of your reality. You need it and are in the process of redesigning its contents. How do you accomplish this?

## Superconscious Mind

The third region of mind is the superconscious or Spiritual Mind and it is from this aspect of ourselves that all perfect ideas derive. It is the realm where you are in direct attunement with the Mind of your Being at One with the Universal Mind, where the plan for the perfect expression of you is laid down and is ever expanding. As you learn to remember and accept that you are an essential part of the Universe, your attunement to your higher mind grows. No one else can take your place or carry out the specific things you will do. In a very real way each person is the saviour of the world, for without you responding according to your true potential as a Spiritual Being, humanity is not complete and the Universe is not whole.

You receive images and impressions from the superconscious all the time, but you are very practiced at ignoring them and the long ages of your forgetting has built up a density that is hard to penetrate. Thus, when you receive the flashes of inspiration or the prods of intuition, you may find them hard to believe for they seem to be too faint for you to hear properly, too simple, or too silly, or too good to be true. In fact, these gentle and beautiful impressions from within yourself, are the workings of your true mind. You may ignore them, however, and strive for things and situations outside yourself which do not belong to you and are merely reflections of the false beliefs about yourself that you are clinging on to, but which in the end bring feelings of failure and unhappiness.

When we talk about higher mind we are talking about knowing, not about knowledge. Knowing in the moment, knowing without proof or logic, knowing without memory or remembering anything in particular. Knowing is instantaneous, direct, simple and devoid of explanations or judgements. Intuition, which is part of the experience of your higher mind, is a knowledge in feelings. In intuitive mode, whatever comes into your consciousness comes with a feeling of profound "rightness". It needs no explanation to be true and when you try to explain it in words it always seems to loose some of the truth, joy, and excitement that you experienced when you had it. Words are never enough.

We cannot speak of knowing without speaking of love. This whole universe is a manifestation of Love and was created from a spark of love, as are we. You are the heart of love. We cannot speak of you or your knowing without speaking of love.

Generally, you experience intuitive knowing as coming from somewhere inside your head, the right side of the brain in fact. This is true but by the time you experience your intuitions, inspirations and profound images they have been fired by the feelings of your heart. Higher mind, knowing is never devoid of feeling. How could it be if its source is the Being of you at One with All That Is, God? And you are love incarnate which is the nature of all Creation. Thus your higher mind and all that comes from it is infused with eternal, ever expansive, Love, whose bodily locus is in your heart centre (the chakra just above your physical heart in the centre the chest). As you tune in and trust more and act on your inner knowing you will experience a change of locus of your mind from your head to your heart. If you are to experience your knowing this is the change that will be most profound. Moving your identification of the locus of your mind from the brain to the heart is one of the big steps you can make in your progress to be at home with yourself and your life.Your heart is the locus of your Divine guidance system. It is guaranteed. No-one else has access to it. It is the only guru you need. The only thing it can do is to guide you to your greatest happiness. Your mind through your heart only knows benevolence. In your actions guided by your heart based 'thinking' you will be setting up a wave around you which spreads far out into the Universe and it will be matched and sent back to you in kind. This is the Law of Attraction and the simple truth of experiencing abundance.

The bottom line is that you have always experienced your Divine Mind even if you have learned to ignore it. You experience it as an excitement, warmth, pressure, swelling sensation, a sense of 'yes ' when something is right for you and 'no' when it is not. With anything that comes from your higher mind, if you listen, there is always a feeling of benevolence and as you go deeper of being eternally loved.

## Mind and Heart

You have to literally go out of your mind to come to your senses. Experiencing your true Mind, your knowing, is all about letting go. Going beyond logic, going beyond remembering and the catalogue of knowledge you have about life. Forgetting and letting go of the past and any fear or thoughts of lack about the future. It is about listening to an internal guidance system which is designed to guarantee the greatest good for you and all others. It is listening to the heart and learning its song which is the locus of your knowing.

It appears that we are all learning a complete reversal of the old ways. You are learning to feel with the mind and think with the heart. In that learning you must trust and follow the nudging, prompting, and guidance without having to know where it is leading. It is in your trusting action that the truth and magic of you and the Universe will be demonstrated. How your actions and the results come together will defy logic every time. This is the beauty of your truth. This is the miracle of living. The only proof you will get is the experience that it works. You cannot preconceive the why or the how without destroying it. Knowing and living just is and can be an expression of your unbounded joy. So use the force and trust your heart.

## Self Healing

As we have seen in the quantum, the New conscious Reality, it is clear that the laws that operate in the Universe operate everywhere from the largest to the smallest field region of the consciousness of All That Is. Everything is energy or energy potential and how energy interacts, as wave or particle, is reflected in all energy fields everywhere. Your physical body system is like a Universe of energy appearing to be held together in a finite time and space reality by your loving consciousness. What you project into it affects how it behaves and how you experience it, and the physical world. You are the Master (from the word 'mastery', or better still from the combination of 'Ma (mother) and 'aster' (star)) of this Universe, your physical body.

Your body is a coherent field of 100 trillion cells each with a consciousness; each linked to all others for instantaneous communication (non-locality law ); each with a memory to past knowing of, not only how to become a human form, but how all other animate forms develop; each with an instruction set of what form and function it is to perform and how this relates to all other cells in the field; each with the capacity for self-diagnosis and the ability to attain balance and the proper flow of energy (eg nutrients, oxygen and water) in and out of itself such that it enhances the well being of itself, and therefore all other cells; each with the power to regenerate and to reproduce itself as well as self destruct to preserve the whole.

For the field to remain fully functioning it needs to be a unified, open system with each component playing its full, interrelated and essential part. Your body was conceived in love, drawn together through your conscious love filled intention to incarnate, each cell with the potential for perfect balance within the whole system. Balance in the whole system results in ease in every aspect of life in the physical density. Any imbalance which affects your thinking of the truth of you as an incarnate Being of Love, affects the whole system. The longer a belief is held that denies the truth of you, the more likely it will be experienced as an imbalance, blockage or dis-ease in your body.

Your consciousness is connected to every cell in your body because it is one of the wave forms of your field. Through your consciousness, you can communicate with every organ and every tissue. Your thought has absolute dominion over your physical body. When there are "holes" in particular parts of the energy field, they will reflect in a corresponding weakness in specific parts of your physical body and they occur in the energy field long before there is ever any evidence of it at the physical level.

Physical ailments, aches and pains and even accidents, bare a direct relationship to the energy movement in your field and are the result of incomplete and misdirected love consciousness. Disease in the cells is the result of prolonged deprivation of life force bought about by unconscious misqualification and denial of the truth of your Being. Your Being refects the imbalance back to you by providing some limit in order to have a life experience that you will greatly benefit from and can overcome through correction. This is especially true now in these times of transformation and change. It is becoming more common place for sudden and apparently miraculous cures from even years of affliction. The instances of these 'miraculous' cures will increase as the new energy therapies, healing practices, cell knowledge technologies, and above all, increased self empowerment and the belief of the power of one's own intent, flourish.

One way or another you create your body imbalances. If you make decisions that leave you stressed, it will eventually create a blockage in the energy field which will lead to a body experience to reflect it. The symptom speaks a certain language, which reflects the idea that you have created in your beliefs about yourself. For example, you may have hurt your leg badly and cannot walk. A likely cause can be your having kept yourself from walking away from something that was affirming an untruth about you. There are no accidents and no coincidences. These events happen according to a pattern and order. The body is only reflecting the truth of the consciousness you are holding in your energy field. Change the field (consciousness) and you resolve the imbalance.

When your inner guidance system speaks to you it speaks in this simple way matching emotion to belief and physical symptom to emotion and feeling. When you tune in to what needs your attention you will immediately be impressed to do something. Whatever calls your attention, will either feel good, or not in some way. You move with what feels good, what gives you release no matter how small, no matter how apparently insignificant. Wherever possible you do not do what doesn't feel good. When you do not follow your knowing through your inner prompting you will feel tension. The more you practice taking notice of what is pressing on you and following the guidance, the more sensitive and accurate, empowered, and happy you will become.

If you do not listen the voice must get louder. The next level of communication after the inner promptings is through the emotions. They are the energy in motion in your body. They are pushing you in the direction of release. As you move more and more in the direction that feels not-good, you will experience more and more emotional reactions that feel not-good. If you make a decision you know is the right one for you, and therefore change direction, there will be a release of tension, you feel better, and you will know you are again on the right track. If you continue to move in the direction that feels not-good, the communication reaches the physical level and has to be dealt with at that level. The physical symptoms will keep reappearing, in one form or another, until the belief behind it is actively examined and changed or until their presence begins to threaten the life of the cells, then the life of the organs and bodily systems, and finally the life of your whole body.

If you heed the messages of your body then the symptoms have no further reason for being. They can be released, according to whatever you allow yourself to believe is possible. If you can create the symptoms with a decision, you are also able to release it with a decision. You heal yourself primarily through changing the beliefs that are negating the truth of you. The beliefs that are negating the loving environment in which cells thrive. Before Jesus healed the sick he asked "Do you believe" He knew that the healing was in the power of belief. There had to be the allowance for removal of the condition of disease by the person themselves otherwise the love of creation that the Master held would not resonate within the sick person for them to be healed.

So in a very real sense we are all in the business of healing. You are the only one who can fully heal you. So healing involves balancing the entire cell environment. It means primarily moving back and into your loving kindness consciousness. It means to nurture the cells, reprogramming them to know your lovingness, gratitude and trust of their knowing. Your body really needs to know how you honour it unconditionally. It involves learning to listen to the signs of the body through the symptoms that you experience. To ask your body for the remedies and trust in its direction. Just as we outlined, in the previous section, the body has its own knowing. The key to knowing what to do is feeling something. Your body tells you through symptoms that there is something to be done and it involves not just a physical remedy. It involves some change in the way you see the world and therefore see yourself.

At present there are probably few alive who do not experience some kind of imbalance in their body. Not only are imbalances inherited, but they can be caused through a huge range of conditions, including the accumulated poisons and toxins we breathe and ingest. Few regions in the world are free of pollutants? Where do you start to redress the balance? Simply by following step by step. We have said that there is a law of your own unfolding and your Being knows everything that you need to be whole and balanced. Add to this the fact that the Universe will bring to you every opportunity to provide the perfect balance if you follow the signs. The signs are specifically designed for you, they change as the time and circumstance and you change.

You have a body Universe that is set up for health and ease. It too will give you the signs. So you start with the most pressing symptoms. What is asking for the most attention? Does the direction involve diet? Then provide it. Does it say "Get some help"? Then go to someone who will give you the most appropriate help for your understanding. Whether it be medical and chemical help or alternative medicine, or one of the newer energy methods, is not as important as your beliefs in its efficacy. Whatever you choose will be of benefit if your intent to heal is strong and the practitioner is sincere. Even finding the right practitioner can be a lesson in learning and empowerment and therefore healing itself, if you follow your promptings. All healing modalities work. It is just a matter of finding the right one for you for that time or problem. The cure is in you not in either the method or the other person.

Always examine the beliefs you are holding that may be associated with whatever problem you are having. If you do not know, then ask within. Ask that you be shown where the root cause is and hold positive expectation that you will be shown and it will lead to the correction of the imbalance. Your successful healing is a reality of these times and will be the direct evidence of your power to create. The stronger the intent the surer the release. If you are stuck for information at the emotional or mental belief level then go to someone who appears to be less stuck. Someone in whom you can sense the Presence of the balance that you are aiming for. They are much more likely to be able to help you because they will be able to hold the healing space for you to step into and gain the perspective of your Higher Self to be able to discern the direction you need to go in order to attain a more permanent balance.

Your healing is literally about your instincts coming from your heart knowing and your bodily reactions. These are what is going to steer you through the now moment and all the now moments for the rest of your life.

Take the pressure off yourself and go easy. It is in the attitude far more than in what you eat that balance will be restored. I have seen many health conscious and/or fitness fanatics quite sickly and unhappy. If your primary motivation is for a greater expression of joy in yourself through your body, rather that the fear of disease and death then you are already on the road to self-healing.

Be as open and flexible as you can especially in the methods you choose for balancing and healing. For example, a good diet is not a religion. It is a choice guided by your preferences and your knowing. It will change frequently as your bodily needs change with the entry of the new energies and the changing needs of you on your path. Listen to the advice of others but use your discernment and take what you resonate with and put the rest aside, for your authority of what is good for you is your body feelings and inner guidance system, your heart knowing.

## Heart Song

Did you know that your heart has a song? With every beat of your heart the song plays to all the cells of your body. It plays the song of your sadness and the song of your joy. Your heart is the music you play to yourself and to the world. It is the signature to which your body responds and takes up and by which others know you. As you open up to the energies of the Shift and the New You tears will flow. Sometimes uncontrollable tears that are washing away the ages of past pain. Tears that are refining the notes of your heart song.

This is why music, and especially certain lyrics of songs, speak to you so deeply. Give permission to yourself to allow the music to flow within you, to do its work of cleansing your body. Give voice to the songs. Sing for yourself, regardless of whether you feel you can hold a tune or not. The music of your soul can change all that. No longer be afraid to fully feel and express the song that is there. The new song that is forming is a great gift for your own total healing.

Your heart song creates a harmony between your field and your form. There is a resonant exchange which frees your energy for all that you desire. It is guiding you to greater feeling and understanding. To greater love and compassion. To greater peace and contentment. The signature of your song flows out into the Universe and is returned with music ever more fulfilling. Trust whatever songs give you feeling, and as feelings are enlivened within you raise yourself up into the highest view you can manage of yourself and life. Let the healing tones of your heart do their work and feel the joyful freedom they will bring to you.

# Chapter 9.

# Being at Home: Connecting to Earth

To be on a quest to make your connection to that to which you feel you belong and are part of but that is greater than you is referred to as the 'spiritual path'. However, you conceive it, the search comes from the yearning inside that there must be something more than the life you know. That a complete state of happiness is not just a dream. The yearning to find your place in the scheme of things and to feel you belong is the quest of the human spirit within us all. No matter how comfortable your life circumstances are there is this longing to be home. To be at home with yourself. Home with family that know and accept and love you totally for yourself regardless of how you feel about yourself. Home, where your inner vision paints a picture of a paradise in surroundings, in the opportunities for self-expression, adventure, and the lovingness and openness of all others around you. In a very literal sense home is where your heart wants to go.

Up until the time of the Shift, to make connection to the One, to the Source, to God, we had to refine and balance our thoughts, emotions, and our body and align them with the Light in order to gain the light quotient in our field to become enlightened. It was like inflating the aura and filling it with light through intention, self-discipline, and purification of thought, word, and deed in extreme. It became a path associated with extremes of self-denial and isolation. It involved a life of love and dedication to the Divine. Often through such discipline the practitioner has gained access through the veil of illusion to realms of light appearance. However, in the austerity of their practices many have lost touch with the Source of their physical life, the Earth herself. We might say that they became ungrounded. In order to reach heaven, home, or the fifth and sixth dimensional reality they grew out of touch with the third, the physical embodiment. It was like being stranded in the light. Only a relatively small number of Masters were able to attain enlightenment in embodiment.

It is generally thought that humanity is in the process of ascending, of moving up in the scheme of things. Of reaching towards a heavenly blissful consciousness with the physical body transformed and intact, complete and enhanced. Could it be the other way round? Could it be that you are in fact an angel descending into a transforming physical realm rather than a human reaching up to an enlightened state of being? Could it be that the difficulty you are having is one of becoming accustomed to the third density from the more conscious reality that you are a part of since before you incarnated? You are coming to earth and the task is more about making a soft landing and establishing a firm footing than learning to fly.

You came to this Earth of yours to experience and embrace the third density and become one with it and now you are learning to blend all the accumulated knowing of your experiences with your fifth dimensional knowing from which you come and know well but have temporarily forgotten. The Shift is the coming of your fifth dimensional reality, blending fully and totally with the third and fourth. We are all being rewired, as so many unexplained body and consciousness symptoms you are experiencing testify to. The veil between the dimensions is fading and you are no longer a human being reaching for heaven. You are a human angel in a biological time/space capsule. What you are learning to do is be in the fifth and blend in the third dimensional experience as one. It is about allowing and enjoying rather than reaching and striving.

So you are taking on a familiar cloak of light and your task is to remember. With this remembering the blending of heaven and earth is assured. So in making your connection to the truth of you it has now become essential to be at home here on earth rather than attaining some realm far removed. It means to envisage what you remember of home and bring it to life here, through your highest visions, imaginations, and intentions, and your acts of love, joy and creativity. Grounding means to take your full place and responsibility in the evolution of our planet. Our beloved Gaia.

## The Miracle of Your Body and its Connection to Gaia

Just as in terms of the New Reality, we are a consciousness field of infinite potential energy. So too is Earth. Her spirit, her Being, known as Gaia is a loving consciousness who holds together, by her intent, every physical manifestation of the admantine particles that she has called forth. All that is physical is her body and her field like ours extends out far beyond her physical surface. Her heart is in the core centre of the earth glowing like a sun. Every part of her has consciousness just the same as our own cells. She too is going through the Shift as we move closer into the body of the Great Central Sun. Her energy gridwork is changing to hold the new consensus reality (hologram) that is evolving. It means changes in her entire energy field including magnetic, electrical, temperature, water and air currents, earth shifts, presence of new life forms and withdrawal of others. Our bodies, as part of hers, are also having to change physically to be in resonance with the new whole. To reflect the new 'holi-gram' (hologram).

We are in it together. Humans are here on this planet of free will to help co-create with Gaia, a new realm of experience. It will happen and it is up to us whether the changes she makes will be hard or easy on us. Grounding is a key to this process of living and being on Earth.

Grounding is first about feeling the reverence and honour for being here. So many beings wanted this earthy experience but you were given it, you were one of the chosen ones. So many wanted to be here in these times of transformation but stepped aside for you. You are a lucky one, though at times you may wonder what a mess you got yourself into. Grounding is about sensing the Holy Presence of Gaia and all that the physical reality is. It is about wanting to be here and dropping the fear for her safety or your own. It is about getting out of survival mode and moving to a fully living mode. And the act of grounding is consciously intending to blend your energy with that of Gaia. A sense of belonging, a sense of being here now is not possible if you have not fully owned the fact that you chose to be here. You cannot feel totally connected to creation if you do not fully accept the honour of being here and the absolute rightness of Nature.

Grounding is the process of connecting your energy to earth and allowing Gaia's energy to enter you and you to fully and consciously merge with her. It can be done very simply in many ways but generally by spending more time in nature, and developing your feelings of the awe, wonder and deep appreciation of your world, your reality.

## How to Ground

1. By taking your shoes off and walking or standing on the earth or grass.

2. Lie with your forehead on the grass.

3. By Swimming or by having a shower or bath.

4. By hugging a tree or by standing in the space between, under the branches, or by sitting against the trunk. Let the peace and stillness infuse through you.

5. By gardening. Touch the earth and building a relationship of giving and receiving with the plant kingdom.

6. Through intention by consciously drawing the light (your life force) down through the top of your head, down your core central pillar of light and out through

the soles of your feet and on down into the centre of the earth. Imagine roots of your life force merging and growing into the light core of Earth.

Any of these activities will ground you. Remember to be present and accept and receive the energy balancing.

The Shift energies mean that your light quotient is increasing. This in itself means that so many people become totally ungrounded. This has been especially true for children as when they are young they are so close to nature and the disruption of sitting in a school classroom for hours disconnects them from their earth source. It is now happening to everyone. Many of the symptoms we described in Chapter 1, for example, dizziness, shakiness, feeling light headed, and feeling that you are not here, can be quickly resolved by one of the simple grounding techniques mentioned above.

Grounding is about being here on earth and wanting to be here and part of the great change. It is balancing the energies above and below. At times you'll feel very ungrounded. You'll be "spatially challenged" with the feeling like you can't put two feet on the ground, or that you're walking between two worlds, which you actually are doing. As your consciousness is making the transition into the new energy and other dimensions, your body sometimes lags behind or becomes disoriented. Touch the ground with bare feet as soon as possible and it will dissipate or at the very least you will feel some balance being restored.

Grounding is about developing a reverence and a sense of awe and preciousness of the natural world that you are an essential part of. When you can sense the honour and privilege of being here you can begin to know your deepest connection to Gaia. Grounding is about taking in the light and anchoring into beloved Earth, through your love of her and all that is here. You are part of Gaia and Gaia is part of you. Welcome home Gaian.

## Your Body Code: The Four Elements

Our connection to Gaia and Earth in our biological space suits is both profound and magical. Life on earth is intimately tied to four elements, Hydrogen, Oxygen, Nitrogen and Carbon. These four form the basis of all organic matter in a huge variety of bonding molecular patterns. There are four only types of compound molecules that make up your physical DNA and each of these has the base of one of these four elements. In the double helix form the four elements are stored and bonded in specific sequences which hold the instructions for energy particles to form the makeup, shape, senses, instincts, intelligence, and emotional pattern, etc. that can develop and which constitute the extraordinary physical presence of you.

The properties of the four elements (Earth, Air, Fire, and Water) give us clear clues, not only to our body makeup, but to the potential for change and growth that we are only just becoming aware of, or more accurately are reawakening to, in the human consciousness. Most cultures have maintained a knowledge and understanding of the nature and function of the four elements. It is only recently, in the modern Western scientific-medical tradition, that a chemical/mechanical view of biology has predominated. Practitioners have not only excluded alternative approaches, but have viewed them in fear, resulting in scepticism, antagonism and ridicule.

### 1. Fire (Hydrogen)

In these times of the Shift many people are experiencing the activation of their kundalini spontaneously as it moves up the spine and out the top of the head.

Many people experience bouts of symptoms that can include any combination of, intense heat up the spine, sweating, sick headache, dizziness, nausea, backache, disorientation, intense sensual and sexual feeling. For some it occurs in dramatic fashion and can last for some days with feelings of being totally out of touch with all that was familiar, of going crazy, and especially of being totally ungrounded. If you are experiencing this energy in excess it can become extremely disconcerting. It is extremely important to ground. To connect with anything that makes you feel down to earth, like any of the aforementioned practices, and to concentrate on daily and earthly things until it has subsided.

Kundalini acts as a cleanser, just like fire, and transmutes, through the fire of the energy, all old issues that you have dealt with either consciously or unconsciously. It completes the passing of finished business.

Your kundalini fire is initiated by your Being in a natural way but can be very frightening when it appears unannounced. It is activated through the connection of the fire of the Sun (the Life Giver) and the fire of the Aurora, of Gaia's core (the Life Sustainer), and speaks directly of the blending within you of the 3$^{rd}$ and 5$^{th}$ dimensional consciousness. It says that it is now time to fully and completely bring your conscious Mastery into this physical life through its activation in your body. The process of your change is heating up. You are to live more fully and forgive more completely, and your inner fire is direct evidence of the increase light quotient you are holding. It is an indication of progress and signifies completion of some level of your processing and the activation of another, in the entire energy system that you are.

## 2. Air (Nitrogen)

Air provides the space in which we live. It is the most pervasive and prolific, yet most elusive element to comprehend, and contemplate. It provides the environment without which physical organic life, as we know it, would not survive. It is the field in which you live and is constantly moving and changing.

The air is over 78% nitrogen, the largest single constituent of the Earth's atmosphere. Nitrogen is a colourless, odourless, tasteless gas in constant flux. Nitrogen appears an enigma since it is absolutely vital for all organic life and yet its presence in excess and beyond delicately prescribed bondings within any organism is toxic and deadly.

Nitrogen is one of the four elements basic to the makeup of physical DNA and so holds vital keys to what you are and what you are becoming. It is absolutely critical and the mainstay of all amino acids, which form proteins, which are in turn the building blocks of all your cells and thus your physical form. Nitrogen is the balancer for it has the holding power to bring your form together by its ability to provide super strong bonds with other element. We could say it is the unifier, the glue, the bonding agent for life. Nitrogen cannot remain isolated and must attach itself to other elements or bring other elements into its unifying energy environment. It reflects the unseen unifier for all organic life.

This uniting relationship character of nitrogen can be seen in its totally dominant place in the transmutation of energy into form and in your intimate relationship with the plant kingdom.

Your body only produces 10 different amino acids but needs 20 to survive, i.e. to sustain your human form. Our bodies do not yet have the capacity to take and hold all the nitrogen bonds in the patterns that the body needs to build and sustain itself. However, the plant kingdom can do just that, take the nitrogen from the air and produce all the other amino acids that are essential to maintain our body. We are absolutely dependent upon plants for our life on this planet at this time in our evolution.

So the next time you take a meal and think about it remember the plant kingdom has brought this offering to you. Think how they have stretched their loving arms into the air and plucked the nitrogen binding it with the fire of the sun, a generous helping of water from the rain, and nutrients from the soil. Honour them and give them the grace of your appreciation the next time you pass a flower garden or the vegetable stand at the supermarket. The magic of plants is in the provision of ingredients for physical structure and balance plucked from the air. The magic of you is in the blending of their gift of love with yours to breathe back into the atmosphere and field around you with your unifying love. Your loving, joyful Presence is the greatest gift to the plant kingdom and as it is given to one plant it is available to all.

Your relationship with plants is a critical part of your connection to Creation. It is there already but needs your conscious recognition to bring the full power of the exchange together. How do you think we can build a world at total peace and harmony? By creating a space for love and you begin to do this immediately you recognise and honour the plants you eat and the plants that are present in your garden or your neighbourhood. The combined exchange of your love and that of a plant creates a powerful space in which the mutual honour of the gifts of each become an atmosphere of love. Walk into any garden space where the plants have been tendered with caring, the peace and love is so clear that you feel you could almost physically touch it. This is the combined power of the love of plant and human in communion, in synchrony, in glorious entanglement.

See what happens to old people, children, grumpy men, or lonely women once they tend a garden space of their own. Their demeanour, their countenance, their face and their space change, settle, and soften. The power of a space for love is as natural and available as the air that we breathe.

Your conscious and full connection to the life force of air, your atmosphere, your space becomes possible with your loving connection to the other kingdoms of your world. Balance, health and vitality return when you make peace with your world by embracing it.

### 3. Water (Oxygen)

Water is by far the most abundant molecule in our body being at least 80%. Earth is a water planet and life, as we know it physically, is present where there is water.

Water is predominantly oxygen that is combined with the energiser of hydrogen. Water is a diluter and dissolver but most of all water is the life sustainer. You can go without food for some weeks but without water for only a very few days. Proper hydration is a fundamental characteristic of body life and the balance and energy exchange of water is crucial for health, vitality and longevity.

Probably the most fascinating property of water is its memory capacity. Water can take up the information of the properties of anything it comes in contact with. It is this property that is the basis of homeopathy where highly diluted solutions carry the properties of added ingredients which can be fed to the cells. Experiments have shown that water does not even have to be in direct contact with another energy source in order to pick up and carry the information of the proximate energy wave. Furthermore, recent demonstrations by Dr. Masaru Emoto show the responsiveness of water to music, written words and thoughts with dramatic changes being shown to its crystalline structure.

The ability of water to memorise and connect with its surroundings and to be responsive to external consciousness energy sources says a great deal about your body which is made from so much water. A more enlightened approach to the environment and energy of the water we ingest will bring profound improvement to bodily balance and health. We have the technology and knowledge to be able to influence water molecules such that, they bond together in a form that cells can easily recognise and assimilate, and we can program water molecules to hold the information necessary for proper cell function and cellular health. New energy and water treatments have already been developed that are accomplishing this.

The implications are great but the importance of these ideas for you is that you have the power to effect what water carries into your body through what you project into it. For example, if your body is 80% or more water and you can ingest vitalised water which is infused with loving intention then that is the message that will be conveyed to the very core of the cells in your body.

Developing a respect and honour for water and beginning to consciously project those thoughts into the waters of earth and the waters you drink is not only strengthening your connection to Gaia, it is affecting the change and evolution of the DNA strands of water. Water too is ascending. As its crystalline structure changes so does yours. We are in fact one body intimately entangled.

## 4. Earth (Carbon)

Carbon is the densest, most solid of the four elements. It is the element that anchors and grounds you to the earth and links you directly to the mineral kingdom and the mineral energy waves of earth. Our vibrational link to earth is enhanced by carbon's relation to silicon, the most common mineral on earth. Silicon is an octave up on the periodic table of elements and we know well that one of the major properties of silicon is that it has the ability to receive, store and emit energy, hence the crystal chip in all our computers. Earth has characteristics akin to being a gigantic silicon chip. It is a store house of information and experience as we ourselves are. The resonance between carbon and silicon is extremely powerful. When you go into nature you are transformed. Stress drops away and bodily balance begins without doing anything. The roots to your earth connection kick in while the harmonic chords set up by these two elements are being played. The more you listen the more it pervades and lifts your awareness and consciousness. Go deeper with intention to hear what earth and nature has to offer and it will speak to you in images, dreams and words if you trust yourself. It is through carbon you have direct kinship with the mineral kingdom.

The strength of your connection by your link to this element becomes even more apparent when you consider your crystalline energy structure. Carbon in its purest and crystalline form becomes diamond. In the previous Chapter we spoke of your developing diamond crystal field, and as you balance your field you resonate more with the new crystalline grid of Gaia. She enhances and influences the growth of your field and you in turn contribute to the harmony of the total Earth field.

The elements of Earth have come together for life. Just look at your planet. Gaia knows who you are, just as the grid of earth does. She has vast intelligence and is in cooperation with your very enlightenment. Just ask the indigenous people who came before you. At the core level of their spiritual beliefs was the honor of the "dirt and clay of the Earth", because they knew our intimate and sacred connectedness to all life.

## A Hundred Trillion Earth Helpers at Your Command

Your form of 100 trillion cells was created by the first fertilized cell dividing into two, and this division happening only 50 times. Every single cell is capable of doing trillions of different things per second and each cell instantly knows what all the others cells do. Your cells have an intelligence, a consciousness that is able to, for example, initiate growth of new cells, to recognise and kill germs, expel poisons, recognise nutrients, play the piano, track the movement of the sun, moon, and stars all at the same time. Your cells, in symphony, mirror the pattern of our Universe and yet are totally at the command and response of your own consciousness. It was your original loving consciousness that attracted the adamantine particles to form at conception, with the open hearted acceptance of Gaia. Your cellular consciousness has the potential to remain in health and vitality and never degenerate until you decide to vacate it, but it responds completely to the consciousness environment that you provide. Your cells can learn to remember and fulfil their fullest potential or they can forget and be caught in survival mode and dis-ease, by virtue of the stress conscious environment you provide.

Every cell has its own brain. Contained in its outer layer are two types of cells. One knows to expel all used and unneeded matter out of its environment and to shut out all that is alien or non resonant with its health and vitality The other set of cells has the extraordinary ability to know exactly what is good for the life and health of the cell and allows in only those substances and vibrations that will bring health through nutrients, and vitality through life force, into its core. The thing about these two types of cell is that only one type can be active at a time. If the cell is warding of a toxin then it cannot take in the food and fuel to maintain itself fully. The stress that we all hold provides an environment in which so many cells are shut off to the sustenance they need and therefore are in a deprived state. This, in the long term, results in degeneration, decay and death, disease and ageing.

When love and joy become a long term condition of the body environment then only health and wellbeing can occur. It follows that it is healthier to eat a can of baked beans when happy than a delicious and highly nutritious meal when stressed. Your cells require a consciousness environment that supports their health.

The cells of your body have intimate contact with Mother Earth. They are part of Her body. Earth, air fire, and water are the constituents of her body, and as we have seen so is yours. Your body therefore can respond precisely and in harmony with any plant, mineral, animal, or nature spirit. Through a profound reservoir of knowledge and memory, your body cells can tell you exactly what will bring health and vitality and what they need at any given time. They speak all the time but most of us are hard of hearing.

Your cells have been listening to you for so long that they have formed patterns of responding that are unnatural, are artificial to their inherent nature, this is why you are slowly dying. This is why the cells are not surviving as long as they should, this is why we have even developed cells which will devour or render useless all other cells (cancer). So your cells need new messages from you. They need an environment of love, joy and laughter instead of stress, sadness and isolation. They need new messages of encouragement to take back their knowledge of health and balance. They need to hear that you love them and honor their capacity for health, vitality, longevity. They need your heartsong to create the symphony of their interdependency and combined amazing ability to work together with their huge variety of talents and functions. As you stop the war within yourself you need to communicate to your cells that the war is over. That you have made peace and that you are now sharing it with them. They need to hear your loving voice just as a frightened child needs the strong caring voice of a parent. Do this often and ask your body for the signals and clear direction for restoring the balances, for providing the food it needs and the care that will bring about its greatest good. Become the loving Master and the caring parent to them all for they are your immediate connection to third dimensional creation and it is your love that supplies the environment in which they will make their transition, their changes (an ascension) for the new crystalline form. A form without blemish, a form that will contain a huge light quotient, a form that will serve you, and many generations to come.

## Deepening Your Relationship with Gaia

To make your connection with Gaia you have to make your peace with her. There is so much fear memory associated with Earth and her power. If you have not had direct experience with earthquakes, volcanic eruptions, tidal waves or storm devastation then you have seen enough of it on the television to know what it can do in apparent unpredictable ways. If you have not felt it personally in this lifetime you will have had experiences of the terror from natural disasters in past life times and the memories of your ancestors have left deep imprints of their horror experiences.

The best way to get your attention is to trigger your fear. Mass media know this well, and is constantly playing out the drama of the "greenhouse effect".

Thus fear of our Earth is embedded deep in our subconscious memories. Each of us needs to forgive her for those experiences in order to remove the fear forever. You need to remove the seeds of distrust and unlovingness you hold towards her no matter how remote they feel. Forgive yourself also for your part in plundering her by your own and your ancestors self-centred needs and fears for survival. Then you will no longer be afraid of the changes that are occurring and you will hear what she has to say about each event of her transformation. It is quite possible through our loving intention to modify the coming earth adjustments such that they do not overly disrupt or lead to massive suffering.

The Earth is changing as we are. She is moving into new energy octaves and we are in it together. She needs you and you need her. You are co-creators. Your intimate connection to earth, through your total and loving acceptance of your physical body when incarnating, is vital for it aligns you directly with the heart of Gaia. She will not destroy you nor see you lack in what ever you need to maintain health. Listen to her. She has so much she can teach you, not just about survival but about living more fully, joyfully and with youthful vitality. You in turn have so much to contribute as a creator, appreciator, and keeper of the beauty and magnificence of Earth and the secrets she holds.

If you can turn away your focus on lack and move towards abundance and envisioning a New Earth, the entire future of human life will change. Change to the garden of Eden of your deepest dreams and imagination. Become a Giaian creating a world of the highest you can imagine and watch it grow. Try not to dwell on lack of food but see everyone fed, no one hungry, no one diseased or infirmed. Focus on the discovery and use of new environmentally clean and inexhaustible forms of energy. They are there in the imaginings of many people and very close to being available. The new world will have no room for lack so learn to look for the possibilities in what is rather than the fear based attention of the old reality.

The only thing that keeps you from knowing the fullness of who you are is fear, adherence to a singular duality consciousness, and the poor efficiency of your current biology. All of it can and will change with better communication between the crystalline structure, and the DNA. As the memory transmission is increased to the instruction sets, the body reacts, and by "the body," we mean the whole human. Freer and more complete communication and energy flow is coming from the new position of the grid system of Earth. Honoring her and your body enhances the development of your corresponding field grid. Recognise and consciously affirm your connection and Oneness not as a servant of Earth but as a Master standing in fullness with her. Remember, we are all connected, your power, the Power of One has an accumulated effect on all of those around you. As you live in chaotic times with chaotic circumstances, like the petrol and energy price instability, unstable and unpredictable financial conditions, threatening social disorder, and widespread individual fear and uncertainty in all spheres of human experience, your ability to maintain your centre, to anchor in your Presence, and to energetically ground yourself is critical. In grounding yourself and allowing the new energy infusion to be a part of your energy dynamic, you not only stop the spinning and feelings of chaos, but you are then able to offer your spiritual support to the growing reservoir of steadiness in the human energy and consciousness matrix. Every time you ground and centre yourself in the moment beyond the fear of temporary conditions, and in the love of knowing your own place in the world, in those moments, you add to the capacity and opportunity of the person next to you who is at present floundering. Your personal steadiness amongst the conditions of chaos allows the changes to be easier for you, and provides a significant opportunity for the changes to be easier for others, if they so choose. Your Presence provides a healing direction for others to look towards in a world appearing to have gone mad.

## The Heart Song of Gaia

Gaia is playing a new heart song. With every beat of her heart the song plays to all kingdoms of her body. It plays the song of her expanded potential and it plays to all of us. The energies entering you are calling your signature heart song to resonate with hers. It calls to drop all the fear of lack and the need to protect your own survival. It calls to take ownership of your own magnificent potential and deepen your relationship with the natural world. It calls for the healing of all wounds and for the dance of the joy of expressing self, unabashed and free.

Her heart song is creating a harmony between her new gridwork and yours. There is a resonant exchange which frees all the energy for dreams of greatness to be made manifest in the natural expression of souls united. Her song is guiding us all towards our creative potential. The signature of Gaia's song flows into you as waves of belonging and affirmation and is returned to her as ever more fulfilling as you learn to express the fullness of your love for her, for humanity and for all beings on earth. Listen to her heartbeat. Hear her song which will take you further into the joyful freedom of being yourself.

When you eventually feel fully that you belong here, when you feel that you are a Gaian and are fully open to the loving, nurturing energy of Gaia, when you take your power as a co-creator with Gaia, when you take ownership for your complete unity with the energies that are your present environment, you will have brought Home to Earth, yourself, and you will be fully plugged in.

# Chapter 10.

# Belonging: Connecting to Family

## Loneliness and Yearning to Belong

In my counselling and therapy practice of over 40 years there are two themes in the life dramas people have presented that stand out far above all others. The first is lack of a sense of self-worth. This is presented in life stories of experiencing unlovingness and unlovedness, of lack of experience of the beauty, and power, and grace of being oneself. The second theme is that of loneliness, reflected in feelings of isolation, not being understood or accepted by anyone, feeling cut off and unconnected to the life that is experienced, and the people around them. Over the years, as a professor of psychology, I have conducted a survey amongst hundreds of students, mostly aged between 20 and 30 years, of feelings including those of loneliness. The majority of students express moderate to high degrees of loneliness and for many it was chronic.

The need to belong somewhere is a fundamental yearning in us all and unconnectedness can be debilitating, resulting in depression, defensiveness, and withdrawal. While you feel the deep yearning to be able to express and feel yourself as unique and empowered, you also have the yearning to connect and be part of All That Is, through direct and intimate contact with yourself, the world around you, and especially to others. Being love incarnate is all very well but love cannot express itself easily when there is no-one to share it with. The yearning to connect is the natural impulse of your essential Oneness with All That Is, and to be disconnected and feel isolated can become an all consuming experience.

The experience of not belonging is part of your waking up. It is an essential part of the realisation that, though you live in a third dimensional reality, this is "not it". You know deeply and for certain that there is much, much more to life than this. You can love others but only sometimes because they do not always appear to you the way you would like them to be, or they do not see you the way you would like them to see you. There is always a "but" in your love because there has to be more. Your connection to others does not seem to last. No one really understands you. No one can fill the void with the love you desire, no matter how close you are to someone.

Your awakening requires of you to stand on your own two feet. It requires you to know where you stand first. Thus you experience isolation because, while this is a necessary part of 'growing up' to who you are, it requires the cutting of all the ties of dependency you have on others for what you truly desire. It requires a divorce from all your human contacts in order to reform them in the light of the new truth of you that is unfolding. This results in the grief of separating and a great guilt of the separation because you are torn between the equal and opposing pressures of, honouring your loyalty and promises to care for others on the one hand, and honouring your commitment to be true to yourself on the other. All this is occurring in your mind and emotions and does not necessarily require any action to break any actual working relationship in your life. It is a process of learning to take charge of your life not to change others. In fact it is only by cutting all the dramatic ties that you will be able to reform the relationships you do have based on the truth of you and on your unconditional love. Love without conditions, love that will be there regardless of how the other is behaving, love that truly allows the other their choices and has no judgement of their worth because your own worth and love of yourself does not depend on their approval of your worth.

The price of this turn around to freedom is the temporary and periodic feeling of being isolated and alone. It is necessary and universal and will come and go as you come to terms with yourself and begin to make your now conscious connection to your new reality, your enhanced state of knowing and feeling.

## The Thinning of the Veil and Sensing and Seeing

Notwithstanding all this, the truth is that you are waking up to the realisation that isolation is an illusion and loneliness is the expression of the loss of connection. The good news is that you are remembering by the very fact that you are experiencing the pain of isolation. Funny, is it not, that there is always a good side to pain when you look clearly and more deeply? You are remembering that this is not the way it should be and there must be something more. Of course there must be something more because there is. A lot more, and it is very close at hand. It is up to you to look, sense and affirm your inner prompting, your more profound and expansive knowing. You become more as you are willing to embrace more.

You are not alone and never have been. Imagine if you were a Master. A being of great love, wisdom, peace, and compassion. Imagine that you were continually in this state of consciousness and you knew how to truly touch others and help them. To heal them from their pain and suffering because you loved humanity so dearly and profoundly. When it is your time to pass over and move to a higher, more blissful and expansive state of consciousness or remain to offer a helping hand to those who were still floundering in their forgetful state, which would you choose? Most would choose to remain. It would be a natural consequence of your compassion and your unconditional love for everyone, that you would choose to stay to help lift others to the place of expanded vision and empowerment.

All those you have loved and have passed on, all your ancestors who have known the love of Earth and the beauty of their experience here, all your soul family whom you know so well in the fifth and sixth dimension and beyond, all the masters and angels who have been present since the beginning of life on earth, a multitude of beings from other galaxies and dimensions willing to offer aid and want to learn and share in this wonderful transformation that is taking place, all are ready and have always been ready with full hearts and open arms. They honour you for the courageous decision to come here and forget, and you are loved beyond words by them all. You are not alone but it has always been up to you to recognise them. They are there cheering you on. Certain ones, your own guides and angels are prodding and nudging you, holding and enfolding you when you are down and laughing and dancing when you feel joy. But the absolute rule has always been that it has to be your choice, your judgement and your move, for this is the planet of free will where you are suppose to have absolute rule of your choices. There are no recriminations, no judgement of right or wrong in what you do. You are loved regardless of what choices you make. They are, however, always present and you could not be alone even though you try very hard. Through holding to their fear humanity has tried for a very long time to keep the door closed.

It is becoming less possible to shut your 'support group' out of your life. With the entering of the new energies and the thinning of the veil between worlds (dimensions) it is getting easier for everyone to make contact with their soul family, their angels and guides (in the fifth dimension and beyond), often referred to by many as 'Spirit'. You are remembering from where you have come. You are standing with one foot in the fifth and the other in the third, taking back your understanding and knowing of heaven and learning to let go of the nonessential aspects of the third. You are blending the two and so sensing and recalling old friendships and family is an essential part of your homecoming and blending the reality of your home with the third density.

As the energy veil is lifting through the blending of dimensional frequencies everyone on this planet is beginning to experience the presence of others in one way or another. For most it is frightening and unnerving and so they quickly submerged and cut it off from their immediate consciousness. It will not go away and these experiences will grow, first by the changing energies that are now becoming a part of the energy environment we are evolving in. Secondly, it is growing because so many millions of people are already embracing the presence of Spirit in their lives that it is becoming firmly embedded in the active working of human consciousness, the new earth hologram. Thirdly, because there is a reawakening of telepathic consciousness in humanity whereby everyone is experiencing increasing capacity to know what others are thinking and feeling, not necessarily in exact detail but in terms of motive and intent. You are becoming more sensitive and more in tune with the thought and feeling world. Along with this you are learning to discern the difference between your own thoughts and the thoughts of others. Your faculties of reception and of communication are being refined. You now have the capacity to tune into other dimensions if you so choose. Everyone on this planet now has the opportunity to become a channel for Spirit if they consciously desire it. You do not have to be born with special psychic abilities. Some find it easier than others but you will be able to develop your experience of communicating with those in other dimensions if you desire it. It is not at all difficult. It takes intent, trust in your own inner feelings and a willingness to include others in your life.

Most fears of this faculty are related to the great suffering of persecution, imprisonment and torture, so many have experience in the past through sharing their sight. Madness has also been associated with "seeing things" and much cruelty still prevails for those who are thought to hallucinate or hear voices. Our ancestors and people from indigenous societies treated people with other sight very differently, often venerating them because of the potentials for the whole community in their visions. The difference between 'madness' and wisdom is a very thin line.

An obvious question that arises when you think of voices or visions is 'How do you know the difference between illusion and reality? How can you know when the source of a communication supports your best interest and one that has a hidden agenda? There are a number of things that are important here. First, remember it is all about your coming of age. It is about you learning to be yourself more richly and fully, more deeply and profoundly. It is about your expanding love and your knowing. Thus all contacts must be in the light of your own discernment and your own choice. Even when letting go to clear the channel within you to improve communication it must be done through your choice. You do not have to accept anything you receive. If you have questions then you must be able to ask them. It is not about being an obedient servant to the Divine but about being a loving consciousness to yourself and all you choose to serve and share your life, your dance with. Thus any messages you get from Spirit will always honour your freewill, and your choices. Communication from your Family from Home is about loving you and honouring your choices. It is about you growing in your own light and so any suggestions or advice will be given as options to consider, ideas to broaden the scope of your viewing, or to provide options that you have not thought of, or have indecision about. No matter how knowledgeable or how magnificent your guides, angels, Masters, and mentors are, you are the Master in training, you are the angel waking up to yourself and you are the one in this dimension. It is what you do here in the present of your own Presence which will construct the future.

Your family from home is very close and are waiting to welcome you with the open arms of unity and togetherness. All you need to do is to listen and accept the "presences" that you feel. When you feel the Presence or have the thought of the closeness of a relative or friend who has passed over, speak to them. Feel them as present and welcome them into your life. Be yourself with honesty. When you need help or guidance ask for it, and expect an answer. For some it may not come in words but in images and pictures, or in a book, or through a chance meeting with someone, but be assured, the more you accept their Presence and acknowledge them the stronger, more real and closer they will come.

## Connecting to Family (Spirit)

How do you know when you are connecting to your family, friends, angels or teachers?

1. You will feel or sense a Presence like someone close by. You may even briefly or faintly see someone, or a light or a flash.

2. You may hear a word spoken that is definitely not from your mind, a phrase or a brief statement that has the quality of a call and with it you will sense that someone is trying to speak to you.

3. Normally, the voice or words will appear to come from behind within you. Like someone is speaking in your head. For some it is like you are talking to you, but it will come from a place that it experientially different from your normal thought processes. For others, the voice quality is quite definitely different from their own voice.

4. Spirits Presence, together with your acknowledgement of them, immediately reaffirms your connection. It enlivens or activates the strings of love that connect you and forms a bridge between dimensions. It literally is an essential step in bringing heaven to earth.

5. You will know that it is benign by feelings in your body. There will be a warmth, a sense of peace or even pleasant excitement. There maybe a pervading sense of gold or beautiful coloured light or even a scent of flowers or incense.

6. Your early contacts will often be light hearted and sometimes humorous. They often come as a prompting to do something that seems to have no immediate connection to reason but if acted upon leads to a synchronous event, a little 'miracle'.

7. To doubt in the beginning is normal and you should expect confirmation of the legitimacy of the communication if you desire it, but do not be over demanding for your family will not indulge you to feed your ego.

8. The more you talk to and include your family in your life the stronger and the clearer your link becomes. By your intention you allow them to be part of your life much to their joy as yours.

As the veil lifts, the energy fields between frequencies dissolves. Your contact and reaffirmation of your 'support' network is an essential part of the reunification of you with where you came from before you incarnated and where you have always been connected. It is part of your reawakening, the conscious reeling in of your faculties, abilities, your truth, and your place in the universe. The New Reality is about your rediscovering, not only who you really are, but where you belong, the field of your unity, your connection to All That Is. It is about feeling at home with yourself and at home with all life in all dimensions of your growing awareness. The reconnection and reunification with Creation is through your embracing the new experiences that are coming to you with your love, with the new belief set, based on knowledge in feelings, that not only is the Universe entirely benevolent, but also that your own progress is totally assured. Your progress simply requires you to use your loving discernment to embrace your fears and doubts.

If you have trouble 'seeing' and communicating with your helpers the difficulty will reside in fear based beliefs you are holding on to. Doubts about your ability, doubts about your imagination and its power, obsolete fear of reprisal through ridicule. There are deep and traumatic memories in all of us of the price paid for being different. You are no longer under that threat so you can let go of all notions of struggle and obstacles. Every person on this planet at this time will be regularly experiencing 'phenomena' that they cannot explain to themselves. Most are shutting these experiences out, denying them, dismissing them. They will not go away. By the year 2012 no one will be able to say 'I did not know'. It will be obvious in different ways for different people that the embracing of a more expanded reality is the only sane choice for a balanced life on earth.

Your courage to embrace and include your family in your life and feel your belonging will enable you to help others to do the same with greater ease. I say again, that every time someone makes a move to their own truth it makes it easier for all others to do the same. This is the Power of One and the connection to All That Is, a fundamental energy law in the New Reality. Your actions, your thoughts add to the human experience and knowledge pool. By bringing the wisdom of your support network into your life you bring it to all humanity.

*********************

## MAKING CONTACT WITH HOME

If you do not already speak with your Helpers you can and it is a very easy and simple process. Every one can be a channel, it only takes a little practice and learning to be able to get out of your own way. To allow the mind to settle and to refrain from accepting that what you hear and see is just your mental mind and a fantasy. Believing is seeing rather than the other way round.

A most helpful and powerful practice is hand writing. To tune in with pen and paper at hand. Sit in a quiet space, perhaps before you put the light out in bed at night. Ask for contact and guidance. Feel, or think as if you are in the presence of others. Imagine golden light surrounding you and invite in whomever you wish, or allow whomever is there to come closer. If you have a question, a problem you are facing, or just a general need for contact and confirmation or validation of yourself then put it forward. Write it down. Then start writing whatever comes into your mind. Do not censure it or doubt it. Even if it appears to be nonsense at first just keep writing. It is just like sitting and watching your hand write rather than making it write. Allow whatever comes to be written. If there are images rather than spoken words then just go into those images and write about them.

Don't make the practice arduous. If the writing is short then so be it. Be patient with yourself and do not expect anything in particular. Allow what ever is to come to show itself on your paper. Write the date on the top of the page and whatever has come read it through once and put it aside. Read it again if you wish only after you have completed another session. This is to guard against you influencing your next session by the content in the first.

You will quickly begin to see a greater depth in what you write as the sessions progress. For some, your guidance will feel definitely from someone else whom you will become very close to. For others the presence will be strong but without an identity, for still others it will be felt directly as coming from a deeper aspect of yourself, your Higher Self. There is no better way, higher way, or right way. How you will experience it is your way. If it empowers you and enhances your joy, your passion, your direction and your life choices, then it matters not how, where or from whom it comes.

Unless you are experienced in this process there are several advantages in handwriting.

a. Unlike just listening in your head or tape recording your voice it is slower and you are busy recording what is said so that any doubts, arguments, and censorship of your mind are not able to intercede without disrupting the message.

b. The slowness also allows you to feel more fully the Presence and enjoy the heart felt warmth and closeness.

c. Writing involves action which affirms the contact in your body.

d. You are able to watch the results unfold and see them out in front of you so it makes the experience very real. It has impartiality about it. Impartial to your life dramas because it is keying you into a more loving, knowing point of view.

e. Writing holds your vibrational imprint, your signature, and is a blending of the energies of yourself with the energy of Home. Just reading it when you are emotionally low will create an uplifting resonance within you.

If you are one who is experiencing the energy symptom of waking at 3am or 4am this is a perfect time for writing since your awareness will be sharp and clear and your angels and helpers never sleep. However, you arrange it, writing will become a source of inspiration and joy to you. The door to the room where your loved ones are waiting is open wide, the portal to other dimensions has been totally activated. It only remains for you to turn around and step inside.

\*\*\*\*\*\*\*\*\*\*\*\*\*\*\*\*\*\*\*\*

All that has been said is about your belonging. The old patterns of individual struggle and trial are coming to an end. In your awakening and remembering you will slowly but surely make your reconnections to those you love dearly and who have always loved you and know you so well. They are beside you and you will know their Presence as you naturally move to the music of your heart song, your own Presence. You do not have to try harder. Just acknowledge and allow and the connections will grow. The more you are prepared to let go of the old struggles, and the beliefs on which they are based, the more the ghost of the veil will dissolve and other worlds will open to you. They will open to enrich your experience and expand your vision. You have all the help you need right at hand. You need only ask and So It Is.

# Chapter 11

# Taking Your Own Power

Empowerment is all about taking back your own power, the life force that is yours and the knowing that is you. Gradually becoming totally conscious of who you are and how the choices you have been making have been governed by external input rather than your internal guidance system, your inner knowing of what is right and true for yourself. It involves systematically removing all remnants of belief that anything or anyone has power to affect how you experience your life and yourself outside your conscious choices.

You have given away your power through your present life, past life, and through your ancestral history. You are now reining back in to you all the Life Force, the Chi that you have given away or has been stolen from you for ages past, and becoming all that you can be.

Where do you start to empower yourself and how can the process be speeded up? It may seem paradoxical but it all starts with an intention to give up trying to work everything out. Lao Tse, the Chinese Master taught that those who try to gain anything through control actually lose it, and those that give up trying to control gain it. The strong and the rigid eventually break but the soft and supple lasts. It is by letting go and allowing that one becomes empowered, not by trying hard to attain anything. It is in a leap of faith. Jumping off the cliff into the unknown. It starts in the experience of stillness and the spaces between what you know as your manifest world. What does this mean?

We spoke earlier of the zero point field, and that all of space is not empty but filled with the nothingness of an infinite potential. Energy waves and particles are continually coming 'out of 'and going 'back into' this field of All That Is. Atoms themselves are energy made up mostly of space (nothingness) and are in constant change. It is in the 'space between' that there is the vast potential of the unmanifest. It is in this space between, in this nothingness, in this gap, in this stillness, that the potential for any change becomes possible, and it is consciousness that directs what becomes the manifest possibility.

It follows, therefore, that in finding your point of totally conscious stillness you will be able to know who you are, what you are capable of, and what you are manifesting. From your point of stillness you will be able see and know the changes you wish to make and manifest them to align with whom you truly are and want to be and become. From a conscious point of stillness, you and your Higher Self will be in full communion, they will be One because your mind, your ego, will not be in the way.

The attaining of the point of stillness, the space between, and the realisation of the state of being in nothingness, has been the common consciousness state of enlightenment for all the Masters, saints, and sages throughout human history.

## The Peace Within

When you experience stillness it is not the absence or negation of energy, life, or movement. Stillness is dynamic, like totally peaceful movement, life in harmony with itself. It can be experienced whenever there is total, uninhibited, non conflicting participation in the moment you are in, when you are wholeheartedly present with whatever you are doing. Stillness happens when you relax inside and are in harmony with yourself.

When you experience yourself in stillness and you give your undivided attention to experiencing the truth about you, you will experience a calm, dynamic peace of perfectly centred abundant life energy. This exquisite peace deep within you is actually the experience of your God Self, or the harmony of oneness felt within you as You. It is the feeling-tone of Being, or Existence, and it is the truest thing about who you are. When you experience the peace within you, you will spontaneously undergo a fundamental transformation in the way you think about yourself and how you see the world. Nothing will seem quite the same ever again.

## Meditation

Meditation is the conscious intention to choose to be with yourself, just as you are, as fully and totally as you can. Making a choice to go into your stillness is probably the most important move you can make to uncover and discover your true nature. It will enable you to live daily life with that new awareness.

As you move into the depths of stillness, subtle and powerful changes will become apparent in your life. These will be both profound and entirely welcome. You will become familiar with the creative Life Force inside you, the energy at your core. The world will look more beautiful because you will be seeing it as it is, without the distorting influence of your conditioning. You will feel different, happy for no apparent reason. It will seem as though you have undergone an important change, a rebirth, as though you've become a new person, and yet you will feel more yourself than ever before.

The major aim of meditation is to move into stillness in order to experience your true nature. To move into the space between, where everything just is what it is, and you can see it as such. The way you feel about yourself determines how you think, what you do, and how you interact with the world. Entering the stillness will change your evaluation of yourself and when you feel differently about yourself, everything about you changes: your thoughts, feelings, emotions and every aspect of your behaviour. You will perceive the specific circumstances of your daily life differently because you'll have a new awareness and vantage point. You'll have less fear, fewer worries, more enthusiasm for life, and you will spontaneously become more effective in all you choose to do.

Entering your space of Being gives you the distance to be able to realistically look at your life choices and remake and revise them. Seeing your life dramas differently and with a clearer and more mature understanding, you will become more willing and able to release hurts, attitudes, and response patterns that were based on your earlier self limiting beliefs systems and that are now no longer appropriate. Being in your stillness is about coming Home long enough to experience the truth about yourself. You have to encourage yourself to do this instead of accepting as true what other people told you about yourself. Others who did not even know themselves.

## How to Meditate

There are many techniques available to bring you to a state of meditation. All of them have their place all of them provide a practice that will take you into your centre of being. There are 'different strokes for different folks' and it is up to you to find one that works for you. As you change, what works for you will change. Many times it can be very helpful to be guided through a meditation by someone else but do be careful that you do not get into the trap of wanting a specific and profound experience and being disappointed when it does not materialise. Guided meditations usually have a specific aim and purpose in their conception but moving to your point of stillness, your centre, and being there can be quite different.

The technique that I will outline is specifically aimed to take you into the undefined and Universal centre of you. It is not the only way but it is a way that has worked for most people I have taught so I share it with the proviso that you must give it a fair trial before you make a judgement of whether it works for you or not. Again be reminded that whatever you decide it is about your empowerment, your feeling of rightness, your going further along the path you choose. It has nothing to do with any power of authority outside you of right or wrong.

To meditate is very simple. It is the simplest thing you will ever do and because we humans love to complicate everything it is most difficult for most people to do. Meditation is the practice of sitting, totally undistracted, with yourself, of simply being in your own Presence and remaining there for an extended period. That is all. Everything you ever wanted will follow from this one state.

The technique is simplicity itself. It involves sitting in a relaxed awake state and watching your breath go in and out for a period of 15 to 20 minutes. Being still. Thoughts, emotions and bodily sensations and external noises are there but do not distract you from your stillness. Nothing else just that. The catch is that you need a lot more help to get to this because you have spent a lifetime being everywhere else but here in the now moment.

## The Meditation Routine

The most important part of the whole exercise is about your attitude. You are meditating for you. It is the time of the day when you are choosing to put everything aside for you, everything. You are doing this because you know that when you are centred you are whole. You know that the only way to be centred when you are not is to get out of your own way. To see from your depth instead of a scattered, fractured and conflicted view. So view your meditation time as Coming Home.

i. **Place:** You can meditate anywhere. Under a tree, in your bedroom, in the office. Low level noise makes it easier but is not necessary. Just so long as you minimise the chance of feeling you must respond to any outside influence eg if the phone rings you will not answer it, you will allow it to ring.

2. **Posture:** Sit comfortably, with the spine straight to maintain alertness, and with your eyes closed. Do not lie down as it is conducive to sleep. Make sure you are comfortably seated.

3. **Space:** It is an excellent idea to create a space somewhere in your home. A small space in your bedroom where you can create a little altar and have something there that is inspirational, beautiful, that reminds you of what you are creating. Having such a 'sacred' space will create a vibrational atmosphere which will help you settle more easily when you cannot be out in nature. Light a candle on your meditation table and a little of your favourite incense or flower essence. Meditative background music without lyrics also helps to create a peaceful atmosphere. None of this is essential but anything that helps you tune in to where you are going, makes you feel good and reminds you of Home can be very helpful. Meditation is about remembering your Higher Self.

## The Practice: Attitude and Breath

1. As you settle down and sit take a deep breath, one that has a sigh, and say to yourself 'I am home'. Feel like you are back from a journey and now sitting with yourself, you are home.

2. Take two or three slow, gentle, deep, breaths. If you have to give another sigh then do so.

3. Now say to yourself something to the effect that, "The Universe is perfectly unfolding and I am an essential part of it. At this time I choose to do nothing

but be with what ever is unfolding. To sit in my most precious Presence and allow everything to be in its place"

4. Just note the sounds around you. They are all part of the unfolding Universe and are in there right place. Allow them to be. Don't try to shut them out. Even traffic noise or a motor mower going in the background, are part of creation. Do not try to shut anything out. Just let everything have its place as you begin to merely watch all that is.

5. Take another slow, gentle, deep, breath.

Now for the next 10 minutes or so just watch your breath going in and out. Don't do anything else. Allow your breathing to flow in and out naturally, effortlessly, without any intervention on your part. Feel yourself breathing. Make no attempt to regulate your breathing or control it in any way. Let the breath go where it wants to. Some breaths will be deep, others shallow. Every breath may be different. Simply experience what's actually there to be experienced. Stay with what's happening.

Every time your mind gets distracted by a thought, something outside yourself, some feeling, bring your awareness back to watching your breath. Let the breath go where it wants to. Just watch it. Let everything else fall away, all that exists is the breath, a river of life energy flowing ceaselessly.

Every time you are distracted, when you notice that you are, you are already back to yourself, so be with your breath again. Do not judge yourself for the distraction. It is like smiling to yourself as you are back. Be kind and gentle to yourself. You are a Being of infinite understanding and patience. Be this to yourself. Even if most of the time you are distracted, whenever you notice it you will be back. I guarantee you that if you do this for 10 or more minutes, at the very least you will always feel more centred, more still, more present, when you have finished.

6. At the end of your meditation give thanks for things in your life and for your amazing body. Give a healing blessing to those in your life you feel are in need. Sit in the stillness you are in and see it as permeating your awareness and your life until you sit again tomorrow.

## Helpful Hints

a) Begin with 10 minutes every day and gradually step it up to 20 minutes and upwards as you improve. Don't be discouraged if your mind is very busy – this is a common experience for everyone. Simply commit to your daily practise and gradually you will improve. Meditation lies beyond the mind in the silence and stillness that practise will cultivate.

b) Don't evaluate whether you are doing well or badly. If you're practising, you're doing well! And don't meditate just to have nice experiences. Meditation is another wonderful step in your journey towards the destination of happiness.

c) Meditating first thing in the morning is best.

d) Try to avoid meditating immediately after a meal because the body is often more lethargic or restless. Meditate before your meal, or several hours afterwards, so your body will not disturb you. Do not lie down when you practise meditation unless you intend to sleep.

e) On occasions it is good to practise your meditation with eyes half closed in order to develop your ability to concentrate your mind more quickly, and enable you to extend your ability to meditate out into your life while walking, working, sitting in a park or waiting for a bus or in a queue.

f) Sometimes at the beginning of your session you can imagine the incoming breath to be pure white light, vibrant with energy and love, and the outgoing breath as a feeling of light and peace. Keep it simple though. The less thoughts and ideas in your mind, the better.

Don't be fooled by the simplicity of this practice. It is profound in its result for you if you sincerely sit on a daily basis to be home with yourself in this way. It will change your life. You will be more of who you are step by step. Your life will change in your own way and at a natural pace because you will be allowing the Law of your own unfolding to work in your life with far less interference from the old patterns as well as with far more insight into your priorities and your choices.

## The Magic of Your Breath

We take breathing for granted as essential to life but something has changed. While for ages past the sages, yogis, and rishis have advocated the vital nature of proper breath for alignment to our Divine nature, their practical routines were often rigorous and demanding. It took much discipline to build a sufficient light quotient to fully still the mind and be in one's Presence. These practices are no longer necessary because the light is entering unannounced by you consciously. Every breath you take is a breath of life force, of light of the pure essence of all that you are. The magic is that the more you consciously take a breath the more the light quotient works from within, out into your conscious awareness.

The magic of conscious breath is that it works to move the energy within your physical, mental and emotional bodies. Every time you take in the light, the adamantine particles, in conscious focus, and breathe out your loving intent, you bring in a part of your intuitive knowing, your Truth. If before you did anything, before you put out any intention, you took a conscious breath you would ignite the energy of your intentions towards your highest good. You are being rewired and your breath, the breath of life, energises your rewiring and begins to allow you to bypass much of the mind stuff that interferes with your knowing of who you are.

When you consider this magic together with the meditation practice and the changes it will bring to your breath, you can see how profound the practice is. The nature of your breath parallels your actions in the world. How you breathe is how you live and how you live is how you breathe. We have said that in your practice of watching, your breath will naturally begin to move to a rhythm of gentle, slow and deep. Breath and mind are closely connected and as you bring all of your awareness into the breath, the mind gradually becomes concentrated and one-pointed. Your attitude in meditation becomes your attitude in life.

Thus a gentle breath will lead to your touch in the world becoming more mindful. A slow breath with rhythm leads you to a natural humility. A deep breath leads you into your knowingness and your capacity for greater wisdom and love. A patient attitude to your wandering mind and all its doubts, etc. will lead you to greater non-judgement of yourself and others, and allowance for things to be as they are without fear or manipulation. And being loving to yourself in your time of stillness brings out an increased capacity for you to express kindness and compassion.

Take a breath.

## From Practice to Outcome

Each time you enter the stillness of your Presence you will be bringing an overflow into your life, into your daily being. It will begin to transform the way you see yourself and your world. It will subtly and steadily begin to permeate your awareness. The more you engage in your meditative practice the more you will experience a pervading sense of peace 'behind the scenes' in your life, even in times of stress. The state of stillness and Presence will become the permanent background in which the dramas of life take on a more transient quality. You will be sensing that "this too will pass'. You will naturally begin to collapse the time line from past and future and become based in a present centeredness.

As your meditative practice develops you will be more and more able to watch your thoughts like a passing movie and not identify with any of them. Not get caught up in them. There will be a profound effect as this capacity enters your normal awakened state because you will naturally be able to identify thoughts and drop those that no longer serve you.

This new found stillness will involve living your daily life with a new and growing inner certainty of who you really are. This is not always easy, and it takes a little getting used to, for it means staying in touch with the deepest truth about yourself in the midst of daily life. This involves continually letting go of the judgments, evaluations, and contradictory opinions about yourself that arise in your mind throughout the day and in your relationships with other people. You do this by staying centred in your peace. You become more aware of any message from yourself or others that points to your feelings of guilt, your unworthiness, or your unlovableness. You learn to disregard inner self-criticism because in your meditative practice you experienced yourself in a new way, as fundamentally lovable, innocent of all blame, and deserving of every good thing.

Having experienced the truth about yourself, while sitting in stillness, though only for a few minutes at a time, you will get insights about an inner truth that you cannot ignore. You will experienced yourself in a new way and now catch sight of your deepest truth, even though you may not yet fully believe it. Part of you knows the truth, but you're not totally convinced, and understandably so. Besides, when you are surrounded by others who are convinced of other things, it is doubly difficult to overcome your doubts. But this arising of doubts and your overcoming them is part of the strengthening of the truth of you and your choice to select your inner guidance system above all else. To meditate, to sit and be at Home with yourself purely and simply is your act of faith. Doubts, arguments, justifications, judgements, excuses, and negative feelings, will all arise from time to time but they are all part of the surfacing of old patterns which will occur and which you will be able to let go of if you trust in your own Presence.

Simply, the more familiar you are with the feeling-tone of your own centred being, when you are Home alone, the more obvious it will be when you move away from sitting in stillness, and the easier it will be to find your way back to centre in the midst of a busy life.

So in fact you cannot take back your power because you already have it. You never lost it. You only fragmented a part of yourself that would not know it was One in and One with All That Is. What you are doing is allowing yourself to consciously own the creative, expansive and all embracing, loving consciousness that you are.

# Chapter 12

# The Power of Your Passion

The most difficult thing we ever have to accomplish seems to be to love ourselves. To love ourselves unreservedly, totally, and unconditionally. To love ourselves, not just as state of mind that holds a set of beliefs about how we should think if we are entirely positive about ourselves, but to truly, passionately and deeply feel the joy, honour and sacredness of our own Presence and Being. This seems so difficult, alien and wrong. There is fear deep within us that it is wrong to even privately honour and appreciate ourselves. Thus we endlessly search outside ourselves to find that love, to find what will make us happy.

## Self First

We understand and even can easily accept the belief that a "good" person is kind to others, willing to serve them and to do this without thought of self or reward. We honour self-sacrifice and make heroes of those who deny their own needs in preference for the welfare of others. On the other hand we find it very hard to justify, as legitimate or noble, the life of a person who follows a path of pleasure and adventure without any apparent social responsibilities. It seems far easier to equate a life of sacrifice of self as of greater value than a life pursuing happiness for self.

The problem is that when we consider our own lives, self judgment gets in the way of our ability to accept ourselves. What we experience, in fact, is that if our needs are not met we become unhappy. If we are always thinking of others and their needs we neglect our own. Happiness equates with fulfilment and fulfilment is feeling full in yourself. Being happy involves your aliveness, your joy and the expansiveness of experiencing what truly "turns you on" to yourself and to life.

Failing to meet your own needs, while holding such strong beliefs that to be good is to think of others, leads you to either search more strongly for happiness outside yourself and in service, or to suppress and deny the feeling and begin to develop a self perpetuating and debilitating feedback loop between guilt and resentment. For example, on the one hand you may willingly and lovingly serve your family's, or co-worker's demands and needs but underneath a resentment of "what about me?" festers. However, the guilt you feel when you do something strictly for your own pleasure, because you label this as "selfish", undermines the value of the experience for you and leaves you with an empty and unfulfilled feeling. You may even add further to this vicious cycle by thinking that your brief indulgence without satisfaction proves that thinking of self will not lead to happiness.

If you think of it, are not all actions we do, in a real sense, selfish? Even when you are apparently thinking and doing something for others you really do it because it makes you feel better about yourself. When you genuinely help another the action itself makes you feel good about yourself. Everyone is self-centred. There is no such thing as a selfless act because all our acts have a payoff for ourselves. We can even get a perverse payoff from the satisfaction of feeling right in our beliefs about ourselves and the world even when they lead to unhappy experiences. In fact, when you look deeper into your negative thought cycles you will find that you seem to have imprisoned yourselves in a set of beliefs that are telling you underneath that you are not of value, are unworthy and deserve what is happening to you. Characteristically it appears that we would rather be right, "I am a failure", than happy. This is at least what our beliefs are telling us. We thus undermine whatever is of value to us by looking for explanations that prove or reinforce our beliefs that we are wrong, are falling short of our ideals, or are something less than Divine.

What if I told you that many of those who have showed so much care, concern and love for others have been privately very unhappy and unfulfilled. Loving God, Creation or Humanity will take you some way towards the peace of knowing yourself, but the only lasting peace and joy comes from feeling the completeness and fullness of loving yourself. In the past few have managed this. It may be hard to believe but Mother Theresa was so deeply unhappy within herself towards the end of her life for though she loved God so devotedly and gave so much to others she neglected the focus of Creation that was closest to her and the most precious, herself.

How can you love, totally, unconditionally any other person without knowing that love within yourself? In the past spiritual devotion has focussed on loving God and this was the way of truly being able to love others. Now in the new reality it is becoming clear that, as you accept that you are indeed God, it is through loving yourself that you can fully love Creation, for you are One and the Same. It is about loving and honouring what you are and feeling the joy and thankfulness for being you as you are.

Jesus said that there were no commandments greater than those of loving Creation (God) and loving your neighbour as yourself. Love your neighbour **as** yourself not before yourself. Think of anything or anyone that you love, can you love yourself in the same way? Does feeling who you are make you feel good? Can you experience this self love even for a brief moment? Can you feel so good about being yourself that you feel like dancing or singing? When you are doing something you enjoy and sharing with others isn't there a feeling of expansiveness, excitement, energy, and joy? Does it not feel sometimes as if you want to burst open? Is not enjoyment an experience of joy?

You see you cannot love without feeling that timeless expansion, that need to share and express who you really are. You, in love, is the greatest gift you have for the world, however you express it. It is the sharing of your own Presence. Love cannot be contained. Does it not follow that if you want to give love you have to experience it, become it? Anything, any belief, teaching, any advice that takes you away from the fact that you are love incarnate takes you away from yourself and who you really are. If there is one reason for being here on this planet it is to experience the fullness of the love that we are. Sharing it is the easy part because it cannot be experienced in a confined reality.

To put yourself first generates for most a fear of being selfish or concerned about the ego having its way and you becoming totally self oriented. The reality is that your life is all about **you,** no matter who else is playing their roles in your experience. There is no one else inside you but you (and the Universe in fact). This is your stage, you are the director, it is your role and your play. You can make of it what you please. You have the freewill choice to view it from the point of director or actor. Creator or victim. So if you are in fact One in and One with the Creator of all, the Source of All That Is, then you are God having a human experience. You are God trying out different adventures of knowing by direct experience and you can experience it fully as an actor, performing so totally your part that you have fully immersed yourself and forgotten who you really are. Alternatively, you can experience from the point of being a human with awareness of your connection to the director that you are, God in action. It is an unkind lie to yourself that says that you are anything less than a creator in the image of All That Is. A dynamic light hologram of the One.

So how do you begin to move in the direction of the centre of love that you are? Simply by putting yourself first. Discovering, following, and exploring your passion. Living more and more your joy each day. Easier said than done of course.

We are what we identify with. If your image of who you are is focussed on your body image then whatever happens to your body, its size or appearance affects you. If how you define who you are is dependent on your family, your friends, then whatever happens to them you feel as though it is happening to you. If your possessions form an important part of who you are then any loss of the things you own you will feel deeply, as if it is happening directly to you, you will experience the grief of that loss. Your world changes when you change what you identify with. If your body size is important but you do not define yourself by how you appear and do not hold beliefs of good or bad on it as defining you, then it becomes easy for you to deal with its changes. If your friends are part of your world but do not define who you are, then, when they leave you, though you may miss them, you grieve for only a brief time. We experience attachments to things outside ourselves as if they were part of us.

It follows that if you begin to identify with beliefs that are central to a deeper truth of who you are, then they become you. This is what free will is all about. Making choices about what we want to identify with. Now it is time to make conscious choices of who you are rather than ones that you have accepted from others. What do you want to identify with, something without or something within? Something small and temporary, or something infinite and grand?

We now have our major clue to loving ourselves. The more you accept that you are **love incarnate**, that you have been created from infinite love and fashioned in love, then that is all you can be. Everything else follows. You have forgotten this but now you are waking up and you need to remember it. Thus your first tool is to remind yourself, that you are love incarnate as often as you can and, to feel as you say it what it means for you. Say "I am love incarnate" when you first wake in the morning. Say it always with conscious intent and feel its impact and its implications for who you are. Say it when you look in the mirror and see yourself. Say it when there are pauses in your day. Say it before you react hastily to someone else. Say it when someone else says or does something that affects you. Say it when you are relaxed before retiring to bed. Whenever you need a reminder know that you have a Divine Self that is you and, that you are now reclaiming your connection to that essence of you fully back into your heart. You came here from an expression of the love that you are and now you are taking back full consciousness of that love that you are.

A conscious intent is important to your success because your feelings are critical to the manifestation of whatever you want. The more you can feel what you intend the stronger and sooner it will manifest. The number of times is not important. There are no rules because it may work differently for different people. You be the judge, or rather the discerner.

To be accepting and patient with yourselves is important because to be love incarnate is to accept that you are a perfect being as you are now. You have always been perfect and whatever you become will be a perfect expression of who you are. This leads us to a second tool in loving yourself and that is thankfulness. To be truly thankful for who you are, what you have experienced and what you will experience is the beginning of being in love. To be thankful is to bring feeling and love to your thoughts. Gratefulness is the simplest but most profound tool for change in your lives. Gratefulness brings the power of positive intent from the source of you into this reality. It is the bridge between your higher knowing and your present knowing-in-feelings. To feel truly grateful for who you are, and to know that you are love incarnate is all that is needed for happiness, everything else follows.

Without each of us taking ourselves first how can we heal the world? As we follow our excitements, our passions and our joys we find more deeply the love that we are. It is through our enjoyments that we can be more real to others. Is it not true that people you love to be with have a zest for life, an enthusiasm? They seem to make life an art of pursuing their enjoyment. Passion, excitement, enthusiasm, zeal, and delight are all felt aspects of expansive, unconditional love. Therefore how can you not be in love when you are following what brings you real joy?

Jesus, a Master of Love, knew the loving Christed Being he was and therefore could feel nothing but love for all Creation. It swelled and abounded within and around him and he could do nothing else but share it with the world, wherever he was his Presence was there for all to experience. Buddha, the Master of Compassion, through his knowing could not express himself without showing the great and all embracing understanding for all beings because he knew himself, he was forever with his compassionate Presence. If you can recognise this in both these Masters you have that knowing within yourself. It was not planted there by someone else. Thus your own enlightenment is a matter of taking full ownership of that which you are and have always been. All else will follow.

## Your Passion

The expression of loving yourself is found in following what brings you joy, pleasure, and satisfaction purely in the act of doing it, the performing of your passion. Passion is not about your beliefs of what is right or wrong. Your passion is about your feelings, what makes you feel happy when you are doing it, and your purpose for being here. Your passions do not have a reason or a set of justifications that make them legitimate. They are simply an essential part of your reason for being here. They are part of the true expression of you and your purpose for being here. They are your gift to the world, the expression of the Law of your own unfolding, your dharma. How can you feel totally alive if you are not engaged in what gives you the real feelings of expressing your Presence, your happiness and full feeling of yourself in the Now?

The simple act of doing anything that brings you joy and a sense of free self-expression is living your passion. Anything that makes you feel good when you do it is taking you in the direction of the flow of your purpose and that of the Universe. There is no need to look for the big task. You being yourself and loving what you do is the biggest task you can do in any given moment. You are not here to change the world but in doing what you love doing you will change everything. As a central part of loving yourself, participating in the things that are fun and enjoyable for you to do should be built into your life. Your responsibility is to discover those activities, those actions in your life that give you the feeling of being more of yourself.

Taking this responsibility involves an act of great courage because it goes against so many beliefs that you have been taught. You have to be able to take the time, make the opportunities, and engage yourself in things purely for the reason of feeling good when you do them. It involves an act of trust and faith. It involves the dropping of the need to justify yourself to others. You follow your passion because this is your own fulfilment and the evidence of the reason will show in your happiness, in your pleasure, in the energy and vitality that will come from doing those things that you enjoy. If you do not try to justify yourself to others they will begin to notice the difference and ask you what is your secret. They will want the same happiness for themselves and if you intend it, you actually create the possibility that they can find the courage, through your example, to try following their own passion for themselves.

A successful life is a happy life and this is your entitlement. But you have to make it. It is your responsibility and your mission to be happy. You cannot wait for the right time, place or support from any other person. The door is open now. You need only make the first step in and your happiness will unfold with every other step you make that is guided by your experience of pleasure and heart felt sense of rightness and fulfilment. Your happiness requires of you to explore what you are passionate about. To break through the old patterns of thinking, and judgement, and to enter into the new adventure of your living reincarnation.

Though following your passion sounds great, it is easier said than done, otherwise you would be doing it now. Fears, doubts come flooding to the surface of your mind and you put the idea aside or relegate it to a daydream of experience, something desirable but beyond possibility within your present circumstance or ability. The doubts are often deeply hidden and unconscious but they sabotage any inclination in you that you can change. To be forewarned is to be armed and therefore the list that follows will help you to begin the process of facing the doubts and fears that will arise as you make the first steps. While you may want to avoid dealing with your doubts and fears, the paradox is that only by going toward them can you move toward the passionate expression of you. You do not have to overcome or resolve all your fears completely, just understand where they come from and befriend them. The overcoming of your doubts, through the action of following your passion and seeing that it leads to greater things in your life, will remove the fear forever.

## Fears and Doubts About Following Your Passion

1. Unconscious fear of disobeying or failing some expectation of what we should be to be a 'good person'. It comes from messages (whether real or imagined) from your parents and other significant people in your early years.

2. Fear of disobeying some rule or 'law' given by a hierarchical organization or authority, eg religion, school or cultural grouping.

3. Fear of betraying your parents who did not follow their passion and were not happy.

4. Fear of displeasing or threatening your lover, partner or spouse by making changes in your life.

5. Doubts from your critical mind that tells you that you are not good enough to follow what you are passionate about, that you do not have the talent, ability, or skill, you are too old and too late, you are too young and not experienced enough, or that you are just not enough.

6. The hassles and fear of confronting all of the excuses that you use to block your real passion: fear of failure, disappointment, not enough money, not enough time, not enough support from others, any lack of any kind.

None of these can stop you from finding your passion and living it if you take charge of yourself. All the energies of your Being and the Universe are at your disposal if you would only make a move in your inner guided direction. A tiny, tentative, trusting move is all that is required to start the momentum of the wave of change to happiness for you. You are the Master, take charge.

Regardless of what you have been taught, what you have been told that you are capable of and what you are not, there is something deep within you that you long to express, that you long to be. It means so much to you, it is unique to you but you are afraid to express it. It is your core essence and is what you came here to express. It may be a way of seeing life, an artistic talent, or a love for something? You are ready to express your highest self expression, the reason you came into this life, into who you are now. Have courage and faith to express it, be it, do it. Do not wait any longer to do what you came here to do. Show yourself. Give to the world what you have to give, to do, to say and to share. Each of you has something special to give. Explore, discover and live your passion and bring to you your full feeling of who you are as an expression of love in action.

*********************

## DISCOVERING YOUR PASSION

### Finding What You are Passionate About

Finding your passion is about doing the things that make you feel most alive and give you the greatest experience of who you are. This is different from your goals in life. Goals are what you aim to accomplish but your passion is about how you want to live your life. How do you go about finding what you are passionate about? How can you break the blocks that are in the way to your living your passion now? I will outline a small set of activities that will help but it is up to you. If you are presently stuck then be willing to stop and give these exercises a try. Treat them as a meditative journey with the intent to discover your own road signs to happiness. Ask for guidance and be open to your own process. You will be looking deeper beyond the old belief nonsense that you have learned well. Be prepared to allow doubt, frustration, fear, anger and sadness to arise if they will. See all this with patience and understanding of yourself but persevere. If you do this you will discover a pathway to your passion. Remember your Being, your Higher Self, your family from Home, and the Universe wants you to succeed. All that is necessary is abundantly waiting to fulfil your living your passion. All it needs is your moving towards it by discovering what you really and truly want that will give you happy experiences and then, make the life choices that will lead in that direction.

As you go through this process just be aware that your passion is concerned with your feeling good and fulfilled in the activity itself. The primary purpose of any activity that expresses your passion is to experience personal pleasure and joy, not to produce, change or achieve anything, though any or all of these will bring additional enjoyment.

There are 3 progressive levels to this process of discovering your passion. To give yourself the best chance of discovering complete them as fully as you can starting at Level 1. If, however, you are willing to commit fully to reach the depth of your passion then go to level 3 first, and do the other two after.

## Level 1:

Take a piece of paper or notebook and write a list of all the things that you have done that have brought you enjoyment and happiness in the past. Be sure to focus on the aspects of the activities that brought you good feelings of yourself. Include in your list.

a. Things you have done recently or within the last three months that you have enjoyed no matter how brief or long it has lasted.

b. Things you have enjoyed doing at school or at work.

c. Things that you have done in leisure and on social occasions.

d. Things you do and have done at home and in your routine life.

e. Any other occasions or situations in which you have felt a surge of pleasure and satisfaction at what you were doing.

Write as many instances as you can and try not to censure what you write, just keep going. When you feel you are done put the list aside and during the next 24 hours try to add to it whenever you can. You may be surprised how many things you do remember.

Now go over your list and highlight those items that stand out. That give you immediate good feeling about yourself when you think of them. What is it about the experiences that have given you the joy?

Are there any themes, consistent activities or aspects of things that you have done that have been repeated in your list? Note these. Is there any way of developing or combining items on your list to form a more expanded experience? Having done this you will be able to see that there are things on the list you can easily incorporate into your life. Intend to start doing at least one of these things daily. One thing that brings you enjoyment. If you cannot do a big one then do a small one but plan to do the bigger one as soon as possible.

## Level 2:

Once you have begun doing at least one thing that brings you enjoyment on a daily basis then you are ready to go deeper into your passion. Finding your passion involves your feelings. It is concerned with doing things that make you feel good in the doing. Though you may be inspired in what others do you have unique gifts to bring to the world for no one else has had exactly the same experiences as you. No one else will see the world exactly as you do. The power of One is the power of your own self expression. The world can change to the extent that you will allow yourself to discover what really turns you on.

In this exercise take an hour of your time to reflect on the following questions and write your responses down in note or single sentence form.

Just step back from your daily self and look at the gems within yourself that may have shown from time to time in your life. This involves asking yourself "What are the abilities and qualities that are distinctive in me?" These are often very simple. Be careful not to judge them in comparison to others. Just list your abilities, qualities, preferences and strengths as you see them. If you get to a block you may find going over your responses to Level 1 will help. But consider the following questions first to help you in your list. Think of things you do that make you feel good when you do the activity, things that come naturally to you.

a.  What qualities do you have in relation to others? Listening, expressing yourself in written or spoken word. Expressing your love and care, as a mother or caregiver, networking and connecting people.

b.  What skills do you have with things? Organising space, prioritising and handling details, scheduling, working with numbers or pictures.

c.  Do you have wishes to work with or have strengths in any of the following? Setting up a good social tone, able to create harmony and a cooperative spirit, teaching and inspiring, helping others to move from dysfunction, or transforming energy spaces (healing, counselling, therapy).

d.  Do you love to tinker or create something? Inventing, developing new ways of doing something, being intuitive with colour and/or style, making through craft, design or in pictures, building or construction, expression through music or dance, gardening.

e.  What are the deeper qualities you possess? Can you easily see things with a heart centred approach? Is it easy for you to take an intuitive approach? Are you very patient with yourself and others and not easily rattled. Are you good at bringing laughter and lightness to others? Can you easily see the larger picture in situations? Do you understand well the simple keys to happiness?

f.   Answer the question "At my best what kind of person am I?"

These questions are only a starting point and you will think of more aspects of your qualities as you move through the list. Keep your responses simple and remember no skill or ability is too small or insignificant they are part of you and should not be overlooked. Invite your helpers or Spirit to expand your list and let you see those aspects that you may have missed.

When you have completed your list you may wish to later ask your friends what they think are your skills and specials abilities. They will often see what you have overlooked or been unwilling to acknowledge in yourself.

To complete the exercise go through and highlight those qualities that you would most like to experience more of, those that excite you and fire you the most at this time.

Once you are able to define a vision of what you truly want to improve or experience in life, you will also be able to come up with many ways of working toward your desired outcomes.

Draw up an initial plan of how you can incorporate more experience of these aspects of yourself in your life. Be as bold as you dare and step out of your box. Plan your first steps and make them. You can make an extensive and thorough plan if you wish but stay open. Be prepared to be flexible for the Universe is very likely to bring you opportunities to fulfil your passion that you could not have dreamt of. Many times people with great ideas and great passions fail to succeed because they have been so preoccupied with developing the right strategy that they have missed the promptings of their inner guidance system and the clues the Universe had provided. Unexpected shifts in focus are characteristically required of us and is the nature of the new energies at work. This is the hardest part, even for people that know from the beginning what their passion is. To expect the unexpected.

# Level 3:

This exercise works to discover your passion and purpose. It involves a high degree of commitment and trust in yourself and your own process. If you want to discover your true purpose in life, you must first empty your mind of all the false purposes you have been taught, which includes the idea that you may have no purpose at all. The more open you are to this process, the more you expect it to be successful, the faster it will work for you. Do this alone and with no interruptions.

a. Take a sheet of paper and write at the top, "What is my purpose in life?"

b. Write any answer that pops into your head.

c. Repeat this process until you write the answer that makes you cry. This is your purpose.

That's it. It does not matter what or who you think you are at the moment. Just keep writing your answers to the question. To some people this exercise will make perfect sense. To others it will seem crazy. Let it seem silly, and do it anyway.

It will take about 15-20 minutes to clear your head of all the clutter and conditioned thoughts about what you think your purpose in life is. The false answers will come from your mind and your memory. But when the true answer finally arrives, it will feel like it's coming from the depth of you. So let it seem silly, and do it anyway. If you persist, after many answers, you'll be struck by the answer that causes you to surge with emotion, the answer that breaks you. Some of your answers will be very similar. You may even re-list previous answers. Then you might head off on a new theme and generate 10-20 more answers. It is all part of the process. You can list whatever answer pops into your head as long as you just keep writing. Ask for help in your process and you will receive it. Stay open.

You will probably want to give up at some time during the process because you cannot seem to reach your depth. Push past this resistance, and just keep writing. The feeling of resistance is normal and will eventually pass. You may also discover a few answers that seem to give you a mini-surge of emotion, but they don't quite make you cry. Highlight those answers as you go along, so you can come back to them to generate new answers. Each reflects a piece of your purpose and you are getting close.

When you find your own unique answer to the question of why you're here, you will feel it resonate within you deeply. The words will seem to have a special energy to you, and you will feel that energy whenever you read them. Discovering your purpose is the easy part. The hard part is keeping it with you on a daily basis and working on yourself to the point where you become that purpose. It would now be appropriate to go through your responses to Levels 1 and 2 above and you will see them in a fresh light. If you have not completed these exercises you will find Level 1 and especially Level 2 will help you formulate an action plan for living your passion.

*********************

# Chapter 13.

# The Power of Gratitude and Forgiveness

To be empowered is to consciously take ownership of your own energy system through conscious choices to be who you want to be and to experience what you want to experience. It is the tuning into the essential truth of you and the vibrational tones that are you. You are in the process of learning to make the music, move in the dance, weave the dream, paint the picture that is the highest expression of you on planet Earth.

There are two primary difficulties you face. First you have been constantly engaged in habit thought patterns that say, both blatantly and subtly, that you are not of value, a victim of circumstance, are always lacking in some way and powerless to do very much about it. And secondly, even though you know this, because your past experience and your history has been peppered with pain, hurt, and unlovedness, the emotional tone of fear, and struggle predominates and has lead you to feel comfortable in retreat, disengagement, denial, and disbelief in your power to create. It therefore is not an easy task to discern what you really want because you are always looking back to what has happened and this has been coloured by negative tones, tones that made you feel less rather than more of who you are.

If you understand this then you are already well on the road to self-empowerment. If you can see that it is understandable for you to feel this way, and that now you hold the compassion of that understanding, rather than falling into the misery and self pity of it, I guarantee you will be able to make the changes that will empower you. It is a matter of patience with yourself, seeing the resistances in you and persisting in a gentle and easy way beyond the points of retreat that will arise.

You can change the emotional tone in your life by simply being grateful. By affirming gratitude in your body by acknowledging what you are grateful for. In this simple act you can turn around to face your reality the way it is, rather than the way you have been programmed to believe it is.

## Gratitude and Grace

To be grateful is to be thankful for what is pleasing to you, that which fires your heart song and makes you feel good. Gratitude and grace are inseparable for to receive Grace is to receive favor and you are favored by the blessings you receive that you see and acknowledge. The short prayer of gratitude that is said before a meal is called 'grace". It is said in gratitude for the food you are about to eat, a gift of love from the mineral, plant, bird, fish, or animal kingdoms. The more you are grateful the more you live in Grace, and by the law of attraction the more you are Graced with the experiences of that which brings you good feelings. The Universe returns a vibrational match always. The Grace of God is to receive His/Her favour and since you are One in and One with the Source of All That Is ( or God) you are living in a state of Grace always. You have forgotten these things and so you will only feel that favor if you can acknowledge it. You need merely to claim your state of Grace by affirming your gratitude for all that you are, all that you experience, all that you have experienced, and all that you can and will experience. This is how you will bring back your heart feeling, your joy, your excitement and your expectation of the amazing, wonderful, and beautiful journey you are on.

You have taken things that you have received for granted for so long because you have taken on a view of the world that focuses on lack, deficiency, poverty, inability, conflict, and misery. If you will state your gratitude for what you do have and that you truly feel appreciative of, then you bring back into your body, emotions, and mind, your love of life both within and without. Through your genuine gratitude you bring into your awareness the sense of awe and wonder, not only of the Universe and the world about you, but also of the amazing body you have, your form, and your energy field. You will begin to see more clearly the awesomeness of the human spirit in the lives of others around you. Every thing starts to be filled with the magic, mystery, and miracles, which have always been there but, because you had forgotten to embrace your world you had lost sight of. This is what being "as a child" is all about. The wonder of being, the beauty of seeing, and the joy of experiencing.

All this with the simple act of heart felt gratitude for anything. This is walking in grace and this is the touch of an angel. Being able to see the gift in everything, including painful experience. Being able to bring light where there was shadow, being able to bring forth possibility where there seemed to be impasse.

## How Gratitude Works and How You Work Gratitude

As we have seen earlier, everything within the universe is a vibrating field of connected atoms, subatomic particles and potential energy. The energy (vibrations) that you resonate and project, based on your thoughts, feelings, and emotions, determines your vibrational frequency and as you broadcast that frequency it attracts to it energy, or vibrational frequencies, that resonate with it. This in turn attracts the events, situations, and circumstances that will match that frequency as your reality.

When you create a sincere state of gratitude your energy is one of acceptance and harmony. You resonate this and as a result project a much higher frequency which attracts to you the situations that will bring more of that frequency, more of that which you desire and that will bring you satisfaction of that desire. You are like a magnet with whatever you are feeling, whether it be love, fear, anger, happiness, joy, gratitude, resistance etc., creating a magnetic force that attracts and draws to you circumstances which will bring a match with what you are feeling. Fear of something creates a force that attracts more of what you fear. In expressing gratitude for any situation you are projecting a force of attraction that draws to you more of what you are expressing gratitude for.

Whenever you resist an event or outcome you place your focus on not wanting that outcome. When you do this your thoughts and emotions are fixed on what you do not want. This creates an attraction force which only serves to draw to you more of that which you are resisting and trying to avoid. Whenever you choose to fight or resist whatever is happening in your life at any given moment, you are actually lowering your vibrational frequency, through your disharmonious state, or imbalance. You begin to attract the dis-harmonious events into your life that you are resisting. You draw to yourself the polar opposite of what you have a desire to experience. Your resistance has placed a focus on what you would rather not have happen, which actually creates what it is that you are focused on. This focus can only draw more of that which you are focusing on.

When you feel gratitude you are accepting of things just the way they are which puts out a very different energy. An energy based on feelings of appreciation of a good, abundant, and fulfilling life. A life filled with rich and inspiring conditions. The Universe will match those energies with more of the same. Being grateful is turning your thoughts to match your inner knowing of the bounty of Creation which then creates that abundance in your life. It is law that it must come to you.

When you start this process it is often difficult to be truly grateful when everything in your life seems to be going wrong. The difficulty is taking responsibility for conditions in your life, accepting totally that it is all the result of thoughts and emotions at some point in the past and that those outcomes are now being experienced in your life.

Since you created them it is possible to change the thoughts and emotions responsible which will produce the desired result. Although prior to understanding how this process works you were in essence unconsciously creating, now you can begin to consciously create more to express gratitude for.

Your perception of something going wrong is only your perception, that is all. It was based on false beliefs and a lack of understanding that everything unfolds in your life perfectly just as you instruct it to do. Nothing in creation ever goes wrong. Everything in your life is a miracle that you created. As you learn to recognize that fact, and express gratitude for every miracle in your life, you will begin to see the life changing power that gratitude holds in creating much more to be grateful about.

When you have developed a point of view that understands that all things work for the greater good no matter how seemingly bad things may appear, it becomes much easier to stay in a state of gratitude. This is also how Universal Laws operate. The universe does not perceive anything as good or bad, it only sends outcomes to you based on your vibrational resonance, and your attitude concerning any given thing is exactly what determines that vibrational resonance.

Make a practice of deliberately looking for the thing that you most appreciate in any situation. This is not to deny other things are present but to develop a view that points you to the value in every situation. Look for the thing you like best and give it your full attention. As you use those things that make you feel good the whole world begins to transform in front of you. You are transforming as you move from lack to the brilliance of you and life around you.

********************

PRACTICE FEELING GRATEFUL

Here is an easy to follow program you can use that will get your gratitude process moving. The exercises are very simple but will immediately begin to change the way you look at yourself and the world.

## Step 1

To start the process take a piece of paper, or even better, buy a special little notebook as a "gratitude diary" and for the next 8 days write down, every day, a list of five to ten things that you are grateful for in that day no matter what it is. Do this at the end of your day before going to bed at night. At the end of the period, go back over your entries and see if you notice anything.

Make an intention to be more aware of what you are grateful for.

## Step 2

Start each day, just before you arise, by sitting on your bed and giving thanks, for your day and for at least three things you are grateful for right in that moment, no matter what you feel or what you have programmed to happen in your day. Also end each day and be thankful for all that has happened in your day before you go to sleep that night. Work with both the good and bad. What can you find to be thankful for in any "negative" events. Stretch your way of viewing things, hassles can be a great teacher. Note things down in your notebook and any insights you have at anytime from your gratitude awareness.

Begin to build the habit of this way of looking in your daily life. Think about all the things, people, places, events, and ideas you can be grateful for. You will sleep sounder and you will start your day more refreshed. As you are moving through your day and are confronted with challenges, instead of reacting, stop and realize that this may be a gift, a training process for you to become more of what feels good and more powerful in your awareness. Start from a state of gratitude in every experience that you have and think about how it serves you and how you can be grateful for the person who just helped you. Each moment in your life that you are paused, instead of worrying and doubting stop and think about what you are grateful for. The moment you receive a compliment, or a cheque, or your pay packet (even if in the form of a bank entry), say thank you. Somebody had to believe in your potential, somebody just bought your service, and that's worth being grateful for.

This practice allows you to bring into your awareness the good things that are happening in your life on a day to day basis, and with repetition, will take your focus off of what you perceive as the negative aspects of any situation.

## Step 3

At one sitting make a list of at least 100 things you are grateful for. Make sure, however, that you feel your thankfulness as you list each one. Avoid doing it in a mechanical way. The purpose is to raise your heart felt energies rather than to complete the target number.

To help you get started here are some examples of what you can be thankful for:

o   Anything to do with your physical body eg walking, your senses, your skills. Your health or those aspects of your body that you especially appreciate.

o   Friends, relatives, a lover, a partner, children, someone that appreciates your company, a pet, neighbors.

o   Possessions: clothes, a car, a house, a computer, a watch, a TV, etc.

o   Your job, or parts of it, any activity you engage in.

o   Food.

o   Particular places and environments, aspects of nature, etc.

o Your talents, experiences.

o Events and situations eg acts of service and kindness from others.

o Lessons you have learned about yourself and life.

You can extend this exercise by including your family or co-workers in making a list of 1000 things you are grateful for over a period of a week. Remind them that no item is too small, just so long as they truly have a feeling of gratitude for experiencing it. Post up a large board and put it in a prominent position for everyone to add to from time to time during the day. Let the list grow without any judgements of the value of any item written. What others write will certainly help you to explore other aspects of your life. Getting others involved is a very powerful way of changing the atmosphere and energy field for everyone into one of appreciation and greater possibility.

## Step 4

Think about what you are grateful for in others and also how you can show that gratitude. Just as you have been inclined to take much of what you have for granted, a perspective dominated by what you lack can blind you to the value of other people in your day to day life. For example, you may take for granted all those who serve you in shops and generally in your community or work place. It is easy to forget that standing at the checkout for 8 hours a day, or packing the supermarket shelves, or driving a taxi, or working on a building site, etc is a demanding task. Anyone who is polite, positive, and helpful is making a real effort for you. They are giving you a gift of their presence no matter how brief. "Thanks" is your acknowledgement of their gift, your gratefulness for the experience of their feeling. Become a little more aware of your heart felt gratefulness for the other when you say "Thank you".

For acts of kindness or giving, why not make up a Thank-you-gram. Design and print a small (half sheet of A4 paper size) letter, headed at the top "Thank –You-Gram". Down the left hand side in a wide margin place some inspirational picture and two or three inspiring quotes you like. At the bottom of the page design and fill a boxed border with one or two more inspirational quotes. At the top underneath the heading write "Acts of kindness are so easily overlooked. This message is to let you know that I have remembered you." Underneath write "Dear" and at the bottom of the page above the boxed border write "Thank you" in large letters. When you are satisfied with the design have some printed or print a couple out at home and try them out.

Keep them in you car or handy when you are out. Whenever someone has been helpful, pleasant and given you a good feeling etc., write a short note telling them what they did or how you felt and either give it to them or place it where it will be found. No need to sign it. Anonymous acknowledgement can be more powerful, it is up to you. You can use the Thank-You-Gram also to help encourage others by letting them know how you admire what they are doing.

You can write a gratitude letter to a person who has exerted a positive influence in your life but whom you have not properly thanked. You may even want to set up a meeting with this person and read the letter to them face to face.

In this way you both develop the courage of being an angel, and touch the other with the truth of the gifts they bring to the world in being who they are. This is a powerful magical practice.

## Step 5

A gratitude journal is easy to keep and can also help you greatly to maintain a positive attitude, because you stop daily to record those things you are grateful for. You can carry the gratitude journal as a small note book with you and write anytime you like, or when you feel grateful for anything. Start the morning off saying aloud, "I am thankful for all the possibilities that the new day brings", to set you in the mood. You can make long and detailed entries or you can just write a few words naming what you are grateful for. Once you become oriented toward looking for things to be grateful for, you will find that you begin to appreciate simple pleasures and things that you previously took for granted. Developing the habit you will begin to be able to penetrate the more difficult and chaotic feelings and circumstances you face with what is of value to you in them. In fact your feelings of gratefulness will become your gauge that you have in fact moved beyond the shadow side of any experience.

Gratitude should not be just a reaction to getting what you want, but an all-the-time gratitude, the kind where you notice the little things and where you constantly look for the good even in unpleasant situations. Today, start bringing gratitude to your experiences, instead of waiting for a positive experience in order to feel grateful. You will not feel the same person you were after a couple of months of daily entry. In giving thanks each day the number of things you will feel grateful for will expand exponentially and as the feeling of abundance grows, so too will you be attracting more in your life to appreciate.

**********************

## Forgiveness and Gratitude

It may be difficult to see why I should include forgiveness in a chapter on gratitude. However, as you go deeper into what you are thankful for, sooner or later you will come to the experiences you have had that have taught you so much about yourself, the 'lessons' in life. Many of these will centre around other people and, so called 'negative' experiences. Experiences you are now glad you had because they have lead you to a greater understanding of yourself and others. A key to your feeling of appreciation for these experiences comes in the wider view of their purpose and the breaking away from your feelings of having been a victim of others. Your freedom has come from the understanding of the choices you made, consciously or unconsciously, and the acknowledgement of the value and gifts in the experiences. Such a view requires you to fully forgive others for any action and to forgive yourself for your part in it. Thus, your gratitude comes from your forgiveness which frees you from judgement of the value of yourself as you were, and the other as they were. Your forgiveness is engendered through your loving, heart felt understanding of the experience.

To forgive is to 'give love for' or in exchange for an unloving act. In being forgiving you are dropping victimhood which says "I am powerless and they are to blame" and feeling grateful for the experience and the gift of understanding and compassion you are now experiencing. Forgiveness changes everything. Forgiveness in essence releases the blocked energy of the past. In fully forgiving you are saying "I understand that you invaded me and that I, have invaded you in a similar manner. We, as well as our ancestors, have gone back and forth, back and forth, each trespassing upon the other, wounding ourselves in lifetimes of rejection, mutilation, pain, torture, heartbreak and annihilation. As I forgive my ancestors for the atrocities that they perpetuated, I also forgive yours, as we have all participated in the human game throughout this experience on earth. No one is innocent, no one is to blame. One can only forgive and in that forgiveness, enter a new reality of freedom and unity.

Forgiveness requires intention. The intent to forgive will bring about the circumstances that allow for the release of pain and trauma recorded in your etheric body and the cellular structure associated with the karma. Generally, your true feeling of forgiveness comes in an act of catharsis whereby you have learned a spiritual lesson associated with the people who provoked the unforgiveness. Typically you will cry many tears, as you understand how your ancestors, and people in general, have hurt each other in one game or another. In the feeling of pain in your heart or emotional body, you learn the associated spiritual lesson; you will not harm another in this way again as a result. As you learn the lesson, then the associated pattern in the field shifts, and you are free to attract a new set of circumstances in the New Reality.

To forgive is to say 'finish'. Enough is enough and the whole cycle of control and power over others stops here. Being right or wrong stops here. Forgiveness creates the space between to dissolve the polarity of good and bad.

How many of us or our ancestors have hacked and hewed our way through human flesh and lives on the battlefields of the past? "Let he who is without sin cast the first stone". What depth of anger and fear leads to these deeds? When will you understand that what one does we all have done and that, as the Buddha said, "When you know enough is enough you will have enough"? When you know that the end of suffering comes, not in retribution, but in forgiveness and your love, then, it will end for you and for others. Forgiving the perpetrator of heinous acts is not ignoring what they have done. It is understanding the pain, hurt, and unlovedness of the person that could lead to such a state of unconsciousness.

There is a perverse feeling of satisfaction among many "spiritual" people that karma will pay someone back for their misdeeds. Do you not think it possible that if a person were forgiven and saw and felt what they had done their own remorse would be almost unbearable? You, with all your knowing find it hard enough to forgive yourself, how much more difficult it would be for them to forgive themselves once they had an inkling of their own Presence.

Is it not possible for someone to turn around completely and forgive themselves? This is the process we are all engaged in and again, each who accomplishes it makes it easier for the next person. Where is the law of retribution then? It is a figment of human imagination for once you forgive what is there to pay back? The illusionary debt is wiped. By our thinking it becomes entirely possible for a tyrant to be fully forgiven and forgive themselves. What would be the payback? All debts are wiped. There is no payment for the deeds no matter how "bad". They have been transformed. This is very hard for the righteous to swallow.

The debt is wiped by wiping the tears. There will be tears. Tears of grief, changing to tears of anger, changing to tears of relief, changing to tears of understanding, changing to tears of forgiveness, changing to tears of gratitude, changing to tears of love. You dissolve the duality of action through the act of forgiveness. It is the power of your loving, joyful and appreciative consciousness that you have given away knowingly.

All debts to be wiped and forgiven and replaced by gratitude. Monetary and historical debt, debt to family and ancestors, to government, and boundaries between countries, and people. The current monetary crisis is a direct result of our debt system. The Universe and the collective unconsciousness of humanity is forcing the examination and elimination of debt. If we are in fact One then how can anyone owe anyone else. It is false in the eyes of creation. Debt says I give you my energy and now not only must you give it back but give back more than I gave you. How can you in truth get back more energy than you gave. It is not possible within the laws of physics. Neither is it possible for someone to give more than they are and yet remain themselves in full. To do so means you would have to be depleted, and disempowered. And that is what is happening at the moment.

Forgiveness allows you the fullness of the blessings of your experiences and empowers you through your gratitude. No one owes you anything because you are full and complete unto yourself, and you are the creator of your own reality. You have set the whole drama up and you are now in the process of scripting another one. Gratitude and forgiveness go hand in hand in helping you play your heart song in fuller measure.

Appreciation is the quickest way to get to the feeling of loving yourself. Being truly thankful unlocks the feeling of fullness of life. It turns what you have into enough, and then into more. In being thankful you are turning to acceptance, you are recognizing the reality of living in an awesome Universe of abundance and benevolence, and moving from confusion to clarity. Gratitude can turn a meal into a feast, a house into a home, a stranger into a friend. Gratitude makes sense of our past, brings peace for today, and creates a vision for tomorrow.

Chapter 14.

# The Power of Intention

## Intention Leads to Creation

Throughout our entire journey in this vision I have frequently used the word 'intention'. This has been quite deliberate. Every time I have used the word I have envisioned an energy of initiation because I have seen that what I intend sooner or later becomes my reality. Any intention I have is the initiation of the seed thought that starts to attract to it the adamantine particles of light that will lead to manifestation of form and event. My intentions are my will-full choices of the direction in which my reality will manifest in form. And since as an infinite consciousness the life I breathe into my creations are initiated by infinite love, the spark of that love ignites all my creations. How the experience of any particular creation feels will be determined by the clarity and focus of the conscious thought of whatever I choose to create. Thus I have also emphasised throughout our journey that, what is happening to us all is that we are waking from our 'sleep', from our forgetting, and learning to become totally conscious.

Total consciousness requires that you take responsibility for all that you see, all that you experience. It requires that you fully realise your power to create and learn how you can create whatever you desire, whenever you desire it based on choices that empower you and allow the space in which all other beings can have that same choice of being. It is a tall order because it means that all that you have experienced has been due to the thoughts you have held and, as many of these have been inspired by unconscious misperception based on a duality view of experience, many of your underlying intentions have not created what you

187

really consciously desire. Your underlying intentions have initiated events, circumstances, and conditions that consciously you have not wanted. Hence, the importance of working with your intentions. Practicing, with conscious, deliberate and passionate thought, to develop intentions that serve directly your purposes, and the direction in which you wish to move.

Your intentions are the initiatory energy that are like missiles of light fired into the Universe to search and find the connection with that with which it resonates. When it does it draws that energy to you, the initiator of that impulse. One thought and a Universal connection to all that is of likeness. How powerful is that? Powerful and scary because it means you had better be sure of what you intend. You are the sorcerer's apprentice, a Master in training, an angel in misfitting shoes. The secrets of the Universe are becoming available, and with them comes great responsibility. But the Universe is wise beyond imagining, for there are fail safe limits to our power to create at this level of frequency. One of these is time lag. In our human past, generally it has taken quite a time for thoughts to manifest themselves within the consensus reality of the collective human consciousness. Unconsciousness has formed a dense layer that has allowed creations to manifest through actions but not immediately through the power of thought. It might have taken up to 7 years for a strongly held intention to become manifest in a person's life, and then for most it would have to resonate with the consensus reality (what scientists refer to as the morphic field) to exist in this third dimension. So there was time for these conscious intents to be modified and refined. Imagine what would have become of our world if our intents had immediate impact through our thoughts on reality. What would happen in a fit of anger?

In Chapters 1 and 2 we spoke about the fact that we are all being infused with light from Home and it is moving you into the stream of a New Reality where consciousness is everything, where we are creators of all that we see and experience, merely through being at least an observer, where we are all connected, where time and space disappear, and where what ever we do or intend has an immediate effect on All That Is. The enlivening of this Field of being means that you are now so much more powerful than you were a few years ago. You can create far more easily and directly. The law of cause and effect operates quicker. What took often a lifetime for people to move through may take only a month or two. This is what you are experiencing when you feel that life is speeding up. It is because deep down in the heart of humanity the collective intends change and that is what is happening, big time, for everyone in all aspects of life.

## Law of Manifestation and Intent

Intentions point to what your inner attention is focussed on. You have conscious intents, but up until you made the decision to take back your own power and your own truth, your unconscious intents have directed your choices. Most of your intentions have been based on fear, lack, survival, belonging, need for love, approval and recognition. Intentions lead to manifestation through the feelings behind them. Love and giving lead to joy, and happiness, to the events and circumstances which promote these feelings. When you are looking for someone or something outside your self to make you feel loved (your out-attention) you do this because you feel inadequate, and less than you really are. Thus you will attract and choose relationships that will reflect the attitudes back of how you feel about yourself. The world is, and will continue to be, a reflection of how you feel about yourself. And thus every event, every relationship will point you towards where you are off balance with yourself, where you are hiding, denying, or doubting your own worthiness and lovingness. It will reflect where you are holding fear and what intentions are guiding your experiences. As you become empowered you begin to change the beliefs and therefore the match of your intentions to those of your inner attention.

Much recently has been said about the Law of Attraction. You attract what you put out. Why this Law does not appear to work for most people is because the primary intent behind their attempts is based on beliefs that they do not have enough. It is a false belief since, what you need you already have access to and more. The intention is based on the fear of lack.

What you put out is what you get back. The energy you give out, based on your beliefs, your emotions, your behaviour, the vibrational frequency you give off, is what determines the kind of reality experience you have because physical reality does not exist except as a reflection of what you strongly believe is true for you. That is all physical reality is. It is literally a mirror of the emotional and feeling tones you are holding.

If you are looking in the mirror and you see your face in the mirror with a frown on it, you know that you don't go over to the mirror and try to force the reflection to smile. You know that if you want to see the reflection smile you must smile first. You know that when you decide to smile, the reflection has no choice but to return the smile. It does not have a mind of its own. Thus physical reality will not change until you do first. If you do change, it has no choice but to follow suit because it is only a reflection of what you are putting out. Likewise, if you begin to fashion your intent on what you really want and know in your heart of hearts, the core of your feeling, that it is so, then, so it is. It has to be. It is already a fact under the Law of Manifestation. Here is a wonderful and powerful mantra you can say after putting out any intention, "And So It Is". The more you use it the more you will feel it and the more fully you will experience your intents becoming your experience.

# How to Intend

You commonly assume that the cause of an effect is the result of some physical act based on some active thought which leads up to that effect. There is an action to reaction chain of events. If you aim to write a letter, then the cause would be the series of preparation steps, like getting out pen and paper, and composing your thoughts to the person you are writing to. However, the series of action steps leading you up to the finished letter is not the real cause. The actions are themselves an effect and the real cause is the decision you made to create that effect in the first place. That is the moment you said to yourself, "Let it be" or "make it so." At some point you decided to write the letter. That decision may have been subconscious, but it was still a decision. Without that decision the letter would never have manifest. That decision ultimately caused the whole series of actions and finally the finished product of the letter. The decision may be from your subconscious, or your conscious but ultimately your conscious intent will have the greater power once you become aware of your unconscious thoughts. Therefore, if you want to achieve something that you have set for yourself, the most crucial part is to decide to manifest it. It doesn't matter if you feel it's outside your control to do at present or if you cannot yet see how you can get from where you are to where you want to be. As we have said the Universe, your Higher Self will take care of that, and the resources you need will come to you after, and only after, you have made the decision, the intent.

To manifest anything you have to believe that it is possible and remove all doubt. The whole process of creating is activated by your decisions, not about possibilities, the hows and the whens. The decision is about "It Is So", your choices are about the actions you will take, which must include listening to your guidance and responding to the signs, and the hows and whens are already taken care of. The how will come about in the easiest and most benevolent way, and the when will be in the most benevolent and synchronous time for yourself and all concerned.

The Universe knows when you are committed or not to what you want. If you say to yourself things like, "I'm going to try this when I see the right conditions or opportunities, when I have enough money, when the right person comes along. Hopefully it will work out alright". This is evidence that a clear decision has not been made. The more energized you are to being successful, the more clear you are committed to your passion and what you really want, the more it must become a reality. When you've made a clear, committed decision, it will open the Universal floodgates, bringing you all the resources you need, frequently in miraculous or mysterious ways that you could not have thought of. Whenever you want to initiate a new goal for yourself, start by setting it. Take the time to become clear about what you want, but then just state it out loud. "My intent is ….. Make it so and so it is"

You do not ask the Universe for what you want, you declare it. It is the seed of your thought, and it will grow as a natural consequence of your planting it in the morphic field of the energy of infinite possibility. You simply plant your intentions by declaring them with all your loving knowing. No begging or pleading just knowing and allowing the creative impulse to work. However, intention is not a force of will. You cannot forcefully will manifestation. Intentions should be done with feeling but also with the ease of knowing. You are aligning yourself with the creative energy of the Universe which just IS, and you are simply thinking and stating a fact of the reality that you are choosing to experience. Not with force or repetition, just with love and ease.

Intend also that what you want manifests in such a manner that is for the greatest good of all. Intentions that are genuinely made for your own good and that of others will manifest in a more positive way for such intentions embrace the fact of your connectedness to creation and the effects of your choices on others.

After you declare your intention, you then wait for the resources and synchronicities to eventuate. With practice and belief they will sometimes appear within a day or two, and sometimes sooner. These synchronicities appear to be the result of subconscious action. Like your noticing things that may have been there all along, but now you see them in a new light because you have declared your intention. But other times they appear in quite an amazing and "out of the blue" fashion. The blessing of miracles.

It takes practice to develop your confidence in the whole process so starting with intentions that are less grand will help you gain the experience in your power to create. It takes some time to be able to trust your own process, remove the doubts and qualifications of old thought patterns, and learn to recognize the signs that the process is working. Often things will happen that seem unrelated to the direction of your intention but experience will show you that when you trust and follow, it will always work out for your highest good. If you want to achieve something, you have to clear out all the "hopefully" and "maybe" and "can't" nonsense from your consciousness. This is an essential part of learning to use your consciousness to create what you want. When you are congruent in your thoughts and feelings, your goal will manifest with ease. When you do not believe in yourself you are using your own power against yourself.

When you decide to manifest a really far reaching outcome like following a lifelong passion, the process will still work. It is just that there are likely to be a lot more steps, and you may be led through various synchronicities for some time before you've reached the point where your ultimate aim can manifest. However, great opportunities are just as likely to occur sooner than later. It just depends on how ready you are and how it will serve your best interests. What first manifest is often the preparatory steps to get you to where you want to go within yourself. If you do not fight it, but follow it, you will be moving in your intended direction.

\*\*\*\*\*\*\*\*\*\*\*\*\*\*\*\*\*\*\*\*\*

## THE PRACTICE OF MAKING INTENTIONS

So your thoughts determine the shape of your reality and where your attention goes your energy to create flows. If you intend to attract the ideal friend, employee or partner, your mind must first believe the person will come into your life. If you believe that it is going to be difficult to find them then you will most likely experience difficulty in your search.

## Hints in making your intentions.

1. Be clear about your desires. Working through the practices in the previous two chapters will be very useful in helping you to identify some of your priorities.

2. Align your feeling with what you want. Imagine and experience yourself receiving what you intend now. The more fully you associate with your intention, the more powerful it becomes.

3. You have to believe that you are able to attract what you intend. If you are having trouble being convinced, research into how others have used their power of intent.

4. Having declared an intention let go of thoughts of how it will or can be made manifest. Have trust and faith in the process, and remember that the field of consciousness (the zero point field that is everywhere) is one of infinite potentiality for creation and is working its magic.

5. Learn to be unattached to what will be the result of your intention and allow your desires to unfold in the perfect time and the manner which is the way of the

Universe. Remind yourself that since you have intended something that it is already being made manifest. The energy of creation has been put in motion by the simple reality of your intent.

6. Know that you are truly worthy and deserving of receiving your intention and stay open to receive it. When something that you have intended does not show up in your life, there is usually a block to clear or a something even more important that is to come that you have not envisioned. You will be tested on expanding your ability to receive. This is especially true when you have asked for the most benevolent or highest outcome for yourself and others.

## Examples of Intentions

You can set an intention on everything you can imagine or dream of. You can set your intention on something small and immediate eg on having a clear ride to work and a convenient parking space, or something that effects your world, your community (social issues), or even global events. You can set them with regards to your current state of feeling something or on something that is deep and overarching such as to feel the fullness of your belonging. Be specific (eg for intentions related to daily and small things and short term goals) or general and overarching (eg. intentions related to your preferred state of being).

Use whatever words appear powerful to you and it helps to say them aloud. Use "I intend...." "I am...." as a preface to what you intend and feel the happiness it is bringing, the growing realisation from your knowing that "So it is".

## Some Intention Topics

o Overarching Intentions: I am love incarnate. I am totally conscious and empowered. I am becoming fully at home and at peace with myself. I am totally balanced in all I do.

o Goals: I intend to find a compatible partner with whom I can grow and have a fulfilling relationship. Have children, get an inspiring job, make a career change, write a book, lose weight, or move to a foreign country.

o Intentions for the Planet and Humanity: I intend to feel in harmony with Earth, to feel more deeply my relationship with Gaia, to leave a loving footprint wherever I go. I intend humanity to live in total harmony and peace together. I intend unity consciousness to pervade all human interaction. I intend complete peace and harmony for all life forms on earth. I intend abundance and plenty to be the human experience for all.

o Intentions for Today: Before you get out of bed, you can intend to have a happy and productive day. Before you leave the house, you can intend to have quality time with your family or whomever you live with. Before you start your car, you can intend to have a safe ride to work with a clear passage. Before you enter your work intend to learn something new or be helpful. Before you keep an appointment you can intend to be calm and the outcome to be the most benevolent it can be. Intend to have a prosperous and fulfilling day.

o Intentions for Personal Action: I intend to say something positive and uplifting to all my family, or at least three co workers today. I intend to turn any negative thought I have into a positive. I intend to be aware of anything that feels good today. I intend to touch with genuinely felt love at least three people today, through a 'thank you', a genuine compliment, a smile, or a hug.

o Intentions for Resources: I intend to be open to all the opportunities for the resources I need to fulfill my passion. I intend to meet someone or be provided with the knowledge which will; help me in my new venture; will help me solve this problem; will inspire me out of my sad mood; will provide the knowledge and technique to heal a bodily affliction, etc.

o Intentions for Skills and Talents: I intend to receive the information, the training and technique for what I want to accomplish or experience.

o Intentions for Release of Old Patterns: I intend to remove all remnants of the belief pattern that says to me that I cannot accomplish what I want. I intend to remove all judgments of others and I am receiving specific and thorough help in this.

o Intentions for Health: I intend to be totally balanced in all I am and all I do. I intend my body to be in balance, full of vitality, youthfully exuberant, and in a total state of ease. I intend the removal of all disease, blockage and imbalance in my body, mind and feeling. I intend to discover and apply a method that will completely remove the root cause of my asthma, allergy, high blood pressure, etc. I intend to teach the cells of my body that I love them and appreciate the work they do for me.

You get the idea. Modify your intentions as you go, getting them to align with your sentiments and the direction you wish to go. They will become more powerful, both in the feeling they engender in you and the effect they will have on the outcome.

*********************

## Using Your Support Group

In this time of the Shift in consciousness, energy potential, and creative empowerment, so much has now become immediately available to us all. We have said that you can create anything you desire through your conscious intention and that the Universe can do nothing else but support you by bringing you the conditions that will enable you to experience the reality of your desire.

You accomplish this by leaving it to an energy expression of you that is at present beyond your full understanding, though you may well be able to sense it. The widest most embracing view of creation you have access to is through your Higher Self, your complete and direct connection to the Divine Source of All That Is. You have access to any and all knowledge through your Higher Self, you need only ask and one way or another you will be answered. In addition, your support group of guides and angels are, and have always been with you. So when forming or putting out your intentions do ask for help.

Not only are your guides there to share their wisdom from their wider perspective but also you have a band of angels and friends from Home who are perfectly able to move energies to align with your intents if you enlist their help and if it is in your best interests to do so and will not interfere in the life choices of anyone else. Your angels love to help but always it requires your asking.

If your intent involves some knowledge that you require in order to go further then ask to be shown what is required. When you find a book standing out at you on a bookshelf, that has just what you were needing, how do you think this happened? The more you ask, the more help your guides and angels will give. Don't forget to say thankyou. Expect your requests to be fulfilled and acknowledge your pleasure through gratefulness. Your joy is your gift to them and they love nothing better than to share in your joy.

If you have not used your angels before now then, as millions of people now do, try something small like getting a convenient parking space. Think of your angels and helping friends and ask "I request a parking space close to ... with the most benevolent outcome for myself and all concerned". Watch it appear. And when the space does not appear immediately or appears somewhere else you may find something else was necessary for it to have the most benevolent outcome. You can ask for anything that involves you. A smooth, safe and uncongested drive, a pathway through a crowd to open up, an opportunity to give a blessing to someone, a reminder to keep your cool in a difficult situation you are having to face, a stimulating passenger to talk to on a long journey, a day with interesting and happy unexpected events, etc. It is limitless and the more you do it, and the more you are willing to receive the help, the more you will evidence the miracles in your life. Then you will have confidence to ask for the bigger things, the things that will allow you to fulfil your deepest intents and the larger areas of your life.

Remember this is all about you. You cannot expect your angels to change or manipulate others but they can most definitely help you to see yourself in a new light and to make more empowered choices. They can provide the opportunities for you to experience more of your joy, more of your freedom and more of your creative genius but you will always have to make the choices first. You will have to decide on what you intend and the direction you wish to go. Your family will love you whatever you choose.

You can ask for help on anything concerning your own self improvement. Through acknowledgement and the power of your intent you can release the beliefs that block you and seem to stop you from going where you want to go. You can enlist the help of your angels, your angels of your grid work, whose job it is to reweave the pattern that is unbalanced in your field matrix. Sometimes it is enough just to ask and it is done. For example, if you seem to be stuck with the depth of love for others that you wish to feel, or you are feeling that you do not truly love yourself deeply and there are blind spots that you cannot seem to get past then ask for help. "Dear angels of my grid work, I request that you remove from my energy field all encodements that are impediments to do with my capacity to love myself and others. I request to void it all and that if there is anything I need to be aware of, for my greatest good, then provide me with the knowledge of it so that I can deal with its transformation. Thank you. And so it is."

There are times when the releases made by the angels of your field matrix will bring the specifics of the artificial encodements to your conscious notice for you to release through your understanding, acceptance, love, and forgiveness. This is the time of great opportunity for self advancement. Help is available to accelerate your growth at an unprecedented rate in the history of humankind. By your intent you can accomplish this and even more with a little help from your friends.

Help is available in so many ways but you not only have to be prepared to believe and ask, you have to be prepared to receive, to know that all your requests are heard and answered in one way or another. Be open to receive.

# Chapter 15

# The Power of Touch

Have you ever looked into the eyes of a murderer, the eyes of a rapist or child molester? Dare to do so in a photograph or on the television. First you will see the hatred. Look further and you will see the anger. Look further still and you will see the fear and terror. Look even further and you will see the despair, the sadness and the misery. Can you imagine that that person has probably never in this lifetime experienced the light of a smile or the warmth of a loving touch? They have no inkling of the fact of love nor its touch. They have only known what their eyes reflect so how could they be anything else than what they are? Can you look with the eyes of an angel and see the frightened child in there that has not known the safety and openness of unconditional love and has not felt the reassurance of a loving caress? Can you pass on a loving smile, without judgement of them and their entitlement of being loved?

You have known the touch of an angel, the love of another, even if as a glimpse, you can remember, and the glimpse has been sufficient for you to search for more. Does this not tell you something of the power of an angel the power of you? Does it not also give you a clue to how you can change the reality for others?

This is the Power of One, the Power of You, to touch the world through your Presence, through your smile, through your loving look, through your touch, and through a word of kindness. This loving touch, no matter how fleeting, immediately effects a change in the other. Regardless of where the other person is on their journey, there is always a fractional part of their soul which will resonate and respond to that love that you give, regardless how they actually respond to you. Love is threatening for many people because it initiates a response in kind within them and knocks at the doors of the prison they have built for their own protection and survival. You can become threatening and their artificial response, the response they are playing out in their life drama, is one of flight or fight. For others, the love of an angel is magical. It can change a person's feeling, turn them to look in a different direction, inspire them to make new choices, or encourage them to be more of themselves, and experience for themselves, the Presence you brought to them.

It is time for the whole human nightmare to end, it is time for the loving and healing touch of the many hundred thousands of angels on earth to have their day. It is time for you to come out of the closet and touch those in your sphere of experience through your presence, through your smile, touch, and words of support and encouragement. Each Presence and each touch will slowly and stealthily dissolve the walls of the prisons of unfeeling, of isolation and despair, that humankind has built around themselves. It will begin to bring vision and hope back into the full consciousness of people en mass. This is how you truly serve, not by the big works but by bringing your loving Presence and touch to others, which will in turn fire their own desire to know and feel more. It is such a simple, powerful plan. A silent and profound revolution. This is the real Secret.

People are waiting for a Master to appear, or the invasion of some higher beings from outer space, or some terrible event to wake everybody up, or ascension to magically transform everyone into beings of light. The Second Coming is, however, the coming of You and your remembering of who you are. You are the secret implants in the human family. You are all around the world in all walks of life, touching others with love and inspiring them to look within and choose something better. You are in every level of government, organisation, social, and community system, in every walk of life and all around the globe. What a brilliant and unstoppable force this has become.

## Your Smile

When you were born your very first act of giving was your smile. Between four and six weeks of age you smiled at the world that was "out there". It was your first gift of being in the third dimension. It was an expression of your joy, your love and your enthusiasm for being alive, for what you were experiencing from the depth of your soul. It was a smile unimpeded by any preconceptions, thoughts or imaginings. It was a beam of the sunshine of you. It was a smile of unbridled, total love and joy.

Why do you think most people respond to babies so easily, look for their smile and melt inside when they see it? Because looking into the eyes of a baby they are looking into the eyes of love. Eyes that say it is such a joy to see you, we are one in this love, I really see and feel you and I love what I am experiencing. Babies look from the eyes of Source and in seeing you their smile shows their recognition of the Source in you and the total joy it brings. You experienced this when you first arrived here and you can experience it again if you so intend it.

When you see a baby smile you quite naturally smile back but what is the feeling? Have you ever stopped to become aware of what this soul smile feels like? Before you read on just stop for a moment and do the following exercise.

\*\*\*\*\*\*\*\*\*\*\*\*\*\*\*\*\*\*\*\*

SMILE PRACTICE

## The Inner Smile

This is a simple magical technique many of my clients and workshop participants have found very effective. You can experiment with it and adapt it to suit your needs.

Close your eyes and become aware and feel the energy of your lips. Now bring them into a very slight smile. Imagine yourself as a little child with a smile on your face, and an innocent and open and joyful face. You may find it easier to imagine that you are looking into the face of a smiling, giggling baby.

Now feel the smile that is forming within you. Do not exaggerate it just become aware of your face and allow the smile to enter. Allow the feeling of the smile to develop as you are aware of your child face or the smile of a baby. Once you start to feel it you will be able to allow it to grow. If it helps just make your mouth smile slightly to initiate the process. That is all you have to do. It will not take much practice to begin to feel your inner smile. It is natural and deeply imprinted within you. You can invoke it whenever you choose. It is very simply your natural response to being here now.

If you are having difficulty feeling your smile, one easy way to do it is to imagine you are looking at a baby smiling at you or two children giggling together. Go to Youtube on the Internet, type in the Search window "baby laughing". Watching one of the short videos will be enough to bring back your smile. Feel it and become aware of your bodily experience. With a little practice it will come back to you.

************************

We call this smile the "inner smile". It is totally different from the courteous smile as a social response to others. The social smile is under the conscious control of the cerebral cortex, the part of the brain related to voluntary movement and thought control. The inner smile circuit is associated with the unconscious and is governed by the deep, primitive brain structures that are connected to your emotions and aligned to your heartsong. This latter circuit involves the basal ganglia which, when activated, cause spontaneous and involuntary contractions of the muscles around the mouth and eyes.

It is nothing like the polite smile of a mouth muscle grin or voluntary smile to the camera. To perform a social smile requires, not just an entirely different set of muscular movements, it does not necessarily involve any emotional feeling whatsoever to produce and can signal the opposite to what you are feeling. The secret of your inner smile is in the contractions of muscles around the eyes that give you your "twinkle," you smile with your eyes. Your inner smile is infectious and when you see someone with a genuine enjoyment smile, it makes you feel so good that you may respond with your own genuine smile. You smile because you are happy, and you are happy because you smile.

The inner smile is the genuine smile. It is a smile that bubbles up from inside, and gives you feelings of contentment. It may require very little facial movement but has a huge impact on your internal experience and the feeling you project and communicate to others.

Go back to the exercise you have just completed. Repeat it and become aware of what is happening within your body. As you smile this inner smile you feel the tendencies for the lips to move and mouth to widen. Notice how the eyes feel like they are expanding (even when you do this exercise with closed eyes), a film begins to form over your eyes. Notice how your chest feels and also how it feels like your heart is expanding, your chest is expanding, your breath is moving to a deeper, stronger rhythm. You feel a flow of energy into your limbs, especially in the wrist and knee area. Something quite significant is happening.

As you go deeper into this practice, as you use your inner smile in your everyday life, there is much more to discover, its overall quality is quite profound. Your smile of love has the feeling of the warmth of the sun and yet is cool like a very gentle breeze on your face. It give you a smooth feeling like silk or the gentle flow of water on your whole body. As you smile you are literally bathing your body in the nectar of the Gods. In Sanskrit it is called Amiya, or 'honeyed dew". It is secreted through your central brain, nervous system, and glands, especially the thalamus. It is made up of your bodies natural pharmaceutical "uppers" like serotonin, and endorphins, the body chemicals that give you the physical and emotional feelings of being happy.

Amiya is your body's elixir for when it is secreted it initiates total body health. It increases immunity, sends messages to all the cells of the body triggering their own memory and state of wellbeing, which in turn leads to increasing proper function of efficient nutrient intake, and removal of toxins and imbalances. Furthermore, the feeling of expansive, openness, and contentment when you smile immediately moves you into a different and more liberating perspective of your life in the present. It brings you directly to your Presence. You cannot genuinely smile this way and take the dramas in front of you too seriously. It is impossible to do. You can smile and be practical about what you are doing but you would be doing it with a light heart rather than a heavy one. You would be doing it with contentment rather than begrudgingly. You would be doing it for the joy of being and doing rather than because it is a forced choice of circumstance.

All this in a smile, all this in a deliberate and conscious choice to own your own smile. And in owning your own smile you can use it anywhere. When you sit down to your meditation, tune into your smile. Smile to yourself and then begin. When you are confused, stop, smile to yourself, and then continue. When you are stuck in traffic, waiting in a queue, having to give a presentation or sit some exam, perform some task for the first time, or just perform a chore, smile first and empower your love, activate your Amiya, your health elixir, your happiness "cocktail".

Your brain does not know the difference between reality and pretense. When you pretend to feel a certain way, your brain produces the chemicals to match and, before you know it, you actually do feel the way you intend.

Right now, while you are reading this, stop for a moment and smile. Really smile with a grin from ear to ear and notice how good you feel. And you can use your smile at any time to regulate your mood.

When you are grumpy and frustrated, sad, depressed or feeling down trodden, stand in front of the mirror and smile, even if you do not feel like it. Exaggerate it, pull faces at yourself and smile a little at how ridiculous you look and yet how understandable to feel the way you do. Now close your eyes and tune into your baby smile. When you feel it has activated within you, even if only a little, open your eyes and smile at you in the mirror. Give some appropriate words of encouragement and thanks to yourself and move on.

It is important to realise how often you do know how to get yourself out of a bad mood but have such a strong feeling of refusal to do so. Who are you hurting by clinging onto a bad mood? You may be trying to punish those around you by acting out your displeasure, but the biggest victim is yourself. Using your smile through conscious choice is part of your mindful Mastery. Owning and using your smile in your life will significantly enhance your life and will return as an energetic expression of your love for life and for all that you experience. It is a simple matter of choice.

## Your Gift to the World

And if you can see what your smile will do for you, you will be able to also see what it brings to others. As I have said, your first gift to the world was your loving, knowing smile as a baby. The smile of your soul, the smile of God looking into the eyes of God, that is the other person, smiling at you in your cot. The difference between you now and the baby you were is that then, you had no awareness of separation, no knowledge of disconnection from Oneness with All That Is. You now, on the other hand, are coming from having forgotten and your waking up gives you the experience of knowing that you know. Knowing that your gift to the world is your love. Your smile is one way you can offer the Love of God, the Divine truth that you are, to others, for it passes through your eyes directly into the eyes of the other and touches soul to soul. No matter how the other responds outwardly their soul receives the gift of your loving smile. This is the touch of an angel, the touch of a smile. Just as your smile triggers in you movement to happiness, to health and wellbeing, so too does your gift of a loving smile put in motion that same movement and energy frequency in others. It triggers a frequency in them that they too already possess. Your smile reflects your heartsong and strikes a chord in the heartsong of the other. When you look into the eyes of another with your inner smile you are looking into the eyes of God, the eyes of yourself. When you can feel with fullness the radiance of that reflection you will truly have realized that we are indeed One. Your gift to others will be the gift to yourself. How simply beautiful is the Divine design.

## Laughter

Laughter is but an extension of the smile to the whole body. It is the unencumbered response to delightful surprise, from the peek-a-boo with a baby to slapstick comedy accidents. It is the response of enjoyment when you see the irony, or the funny side to a life drama that is taken to extremes. It is your whole body reacting with release and relief to the joke that you are playing on yourself when you have taken yourself too seriously.

From time to time in my counseling work I have been in a situation where during a session of deep and emotional outpouring from a client I have felt a laugh arise within me, a laugh that will not be dismissed. The client is deep in the emotions of their trauma and all I can experience is this uncontrollable mirth. The more I try to suppress it the more powerful it becomes until I can no longer hold back and I begin an uncontrollable laughter. The more I try to stifle the laugh the more it becomes uncontrollable. Of course, the client is at first startled. I apologise, with the tears of laughter running down my cheeks, but it will not go away. The protest of the client that "It is not funny" is said with a half grin. Then as I ask them to continue, stifling my giggles, they begin to laugh in the same uncontrollable way as they continue to relate their horror story. In the end we are both laughing unreservedly. When our laughter subsides the client is in a totally different frame of mind and feeling, and more often than not can easily find their way through the dilemma they originally presented. The laughter allowed the person to move to their centre where they were more than capable of seeing a clearer way through their problem.

Laughter brings the focus away from anger, guilt, stress and negative emotions but is more than a mere distraction. Humor gives you a more lighthearted perspective, a distancing to the problems, a centering back to your own Presence, and helps you view events as passing shadows in the play of life, thereby making them less threatening and more like opportunities in which to grow.

Like tears, laughter has a cleansing effect as well as providing a physical and emotional release. Laughter increases the level of health in a similar way to a smile through increased secretion of Amiya. Laughter increases the number of antibody producing cells and enhances the effectiveness of T cells which leads to a stronger immune system, as well as fewer physical effects of stress.

Laughter immediately connects you in with others and is very contagious. Whenever someone is laughing fully and uncontrollably see how it brings a smile to everyone in earshot. When I have got the giggles during a heartfelt outpouring in encounter group settings it has always ended in uproarious laughter spreading to all group members. Tears and aching sides are the result and it has been an empowering turning point for all participants. Bringing more laughter into your life will help others around you to laugh more, and contract the Amiya "virus". Realize also that just as you can contract it from others, your family from Home also enjoys so much the song of your laughter.

## The Touch of an Angel

It is time to be aware of your power to effect change in yourself and change in others. Do you remember what it feels like for someone to give you a reassuring touch on the shoulder, to hold or caress your hand in order to give you their support, or to have a warm and giving hug from someone? These touches move you, they initiate a wave of relief throughout your body and the whole of you naturally responds to the touch. You may immediately put up a barrier of resistance or experience a deep sadness or rising joy but you cannot be unaffected. Your loving touch, like the smile works from the inside out. It takes the mind by surprise because its effects have already been felt, recorded and responded to in the heart.

A touch of genuine unconditional love is so powerful and basic to our natural state of being in a physical body, that its effect bypasses all barriers and triggers the truth feelings within us all. It says deep within that "it is all right", "all is well", "you are loved beyond words". A loving hug calls forth the heart song, which in turn, initiates whatever you are holding back within yourself. This is why when you hug someone in recognition for the joy you feel being in their Presence, or because you sense some pain in them and it is your way of communicating they are loved and it is all right, the other may be moved to tears. An unsuspected and freely given touch has the magic of liberating both you and the recipient into the symphony of your heartsongs entwined; of your feeling of connection; of your feelings of common and joyful reunion. Loving touch is a blending of fields and in that exchange you share the knowing of your journeys and the expansion of the world wide web of Love.

This is, dare I say, the overarching passion of an angel. To be the Touch of Love. It comes in whatever way you naturally want to express an overwhelming impulse that says "How can I give to you, I love you". And as an angel you do this not to be a good person, not in order to serve and please others, but because giving makes you feel more of who you are, more joy, more excitement, more enthusiasm, more alive.

Without touch humans die inside. Very young infants quickly become withdrawn and listless, vulnerable to disease and mortality. Touch deprived adults have lost their feeling tone and become over analytical or emotionally blunted, they commonly have lost their sense feeling. It is touch deprivation that is likely to be the most significant contributor to male aggression and depression. Have you hugged a man lately?

The human need for loving touch, and the fact that commonly people are deprived to some degree, has resulted in so many games of control and manipulation between men with women throughout the ages. Our preoccupation with sexual contact reflects the need to connect human to human but in our desperation for touch and increased feeling we have misconstrued the act of joining in love with the need to blend in harmony and openness to all our family and humanity as a whole. To embrace the world, and to be in love with humanity.

Touch is as natural and essential to our current life as it has ever been, so perhaps your touch, as an emissary of love, will be the liberating force that will open the heart of the person in front of you. You will never know unless you dare.

There are countless instances where the power of even a single touch has brought about change in a person's life, though mostly you will not know the full impact of your loving actions. For example, I was at a lunch time open air meeting on University campus one time, at the beginning of a new academic year. Students and various staff were seated on the grass amphitheatre listening. I had to leave before it finished and as I walked up the grass mound between various spectators sitting I passed a student whom I recognized as being in one of my classes. I stopped for a moment, put my hand on his shoulder and asked how he was and what he thought of the speaker. I smiled, and I left and continued to my next destination. It was two months later when the same student came to me after class. He told me that he had come from Australia to be in our particular Degree program in New Zealand, and was making a career change. He arrived, knew no one, and at the time I spoke to him he was very lonely and depressed. He was seriously considering that he had made the wrong move and that he should return to Australia. He said that my touch and acknowledgement of him had made him think that maybe he should give it a little more time before he made a final decision and that he should be a little more positive about his move. From that point on his life began to change. He found friends and an opportunity to move into a more enjoyable living setting. His classes were challenging but he could now see the larger picture. He wanted me to know and to thank me for my caring and genuine response to him. How powerful is that. Just a touch on the shoulder and a kind word. It cost me nothing but feeling the joy of the brief contact with him and look what he did with it.

Just imagine, every time you touch someone, you give them a hug, or hold their hand, or share a kind and encouraging word, you call out an opportunity for them to take their own power, to play their own heartsong. How awesome if you dare to do it. If you dare to put aside your embarrassment of how you feel or what the other will think of you. If you want to give to someone why not a touch, without words it is enough, if done in love it is enough, if you are an angel it is enough. Enough to open their heart, enough to remind them that they are loved without reserve, enough to start a chain reaction. Enough for them to see that maybe it is alright being here, maybe there is hope, maybe people are not all out to get you, and maybe "I can dream my dreams of freedom, joy, and dignity and value myself and life again". What a magical gift.

Chapter 16

# Unlimited Potential of Your Becoming

## It is Your Turn

One of the great contributions of Chinese Cosmology to the knowledge of humankind is the 'I Ching', the book of Changes. It is used as an advisor for making life choices and it is about the nature of reality and the perpetual cycles of movement and the constancy of change. So when you ask the oracle about some problem or question in your life it will respond with an open ended picture that always leaves you choice. It will not give you a specific direction because your future can only be determined by the choices you make and each choice makes available the potential for new beginnings. Thus, for the I Ching there are no 'beginnings' and no 'ends' there is only 'before completion' and 'after completion', because nature moves as a never ending cycle or circle. Your life progress moves as a never ending spiral. You have no beginning and there is no end and you are always turning as you move forward moving around the eternal bend to discover what is next. And amazingly this is how we have named the place where we live, the 'Universe', meaning 'Uni', one and 'verse', turn. The key we have hidden in our language, and there are so many, is that to be you, all you have to do is to make a turn. Turn around, look another way, look within instead of without, look for the light instead of fixating on the shadow, look forward instead of always looking back, drift downstream with ease instead of trying to row upstream or tread water in one place. Look deeper into your own eyes to see that you are God rather than the potential for evil ('evil' spelled backwards is 'live') and unknowingness.

How you experience life depends entirely on your own point of view and regardless of what you have 'suffered', what excuses you make, who you blame, it is only the way you have perceived your life so far. They are your thoughts, your feelings, there is no one else in there but you. And as we have seen, you have so much power to make a turn around, a change in your way of looking, if you so choose. If you wish to choose to remain feeling powerless, feeling as if you have no choice then, you have the right and the freewill to do so. No judgement, it is just your choice for as long as you wish it to be. Isn't that crazy? Why would you choose to not have any choice in your life and not move in the direction you wish to go? It would only be because you enjoy being miserable, or that you hold some perverse belief that says you are supposed to suffer.

Well the Consciousness Shift is about change and choice. You chose to come here, at this time of accelerated growth of Earth and all her inhabitants. You came knowing that the heat would be on and there would be some unprecedented opportunities to experience, learn, and make a special contribution of the unique gift of you to the whole blueprint of Earth. So it does not make sense to then say 'I have no choice'. The Shift is you, and if you want to be a part of it you have to be willing and courageous enough to shift, to turn and walk on in love. Ironically then in fact, you have no choice but to make choices, without knowing where they will lead but becoming excited by the possibilities. This is what becoming is. 'Being' in the 'coming' of you. Dear beloved reader, you are the greatest gift you could bring to the world. You have been chosen to come here, amongst countless souls, because of something unique that you hold, you carry in your Presence. You do not even have to know exactly what it is. You just need to be here, at home with yourself, and explore, experience, and enjoy your life as fully as you are capable of. That's all. No rules, no buts, or shoulds, or can'ts. Just you saying "yes" to life and the Universe saying "yes and welcome back" to you.

## You are On the Move

Yes the consciousness of humankind is well and truly on the move. The momentum is gathering. There will be very little linear time between the changes that are happening in the consciousness of people. Humanity has long suffered the combined fetters of their forgetting, accumulated pain and self abuse, and the misguided and manipulated interference from power mongers and uninvited visitors. The critical mass of human consciousness has said "enough is enough" and slowly and surely the self imposed bonds are being severed and the prison walls demolished. Love will accomplish all this and the only requirement for the great transformation is that you take back the memory of your Love as often and wherever you can. Your only service then will be to show that growing, all encompassing love of yourself and Creation, through your life, through your Presence. That will be the beacon that will galvanise others into searching for themselves for that same reality.

Each of you has the power of the "hundredth monkey" because the consciousness of humanity is ready for Love. Now, as one voice, humanity has consciously and unconsciously said "No more" to blindness, "No more" to the pain of powerlessness, "No more" to separation and loneliness, and "Bring on the Love of Creation". The collective consciousness is now saying loudly, so loudly that it is reverberating throughout the galaxy, "I want to know what love is first hand". No more seeing Love in a chosen few and holding on desperately to beliefs that say "If I do the right thing, one day the rewards will come". No more promises.

Experience is the only thing that will assuage the yearning that has arisen in the hearts of humanity. Where will that come from? The experience of Love will come from within and for most will be sparked by the Touch of an angel in human form and fired by their own inner yearning. And it will not be enough to have tasted it. Every being on this planet once being exposed to Love will not stop until they attain the fullness of that Love within themselves. It will spread like an incredible Ease, an amazing Presence and an Infinite belonging.

One Touch is enough. Every time you meet anyone, one touch, one look, one smile, one word of kindness, one peace filled breath is all that is required and it is what angels do. Angels are obsessed with the passion to build Paradise wherever they go. A place of beauty, tranquillity, unity, and for the expression of joy in an infinite variety of colours and expressions. A place where all beings are able to fully express the truth of who they are and co create the highest of all that they can envisage.

Your shift is about your love which you must feel yourself. It is not a belief it is an energy, a power, an all embracing, all encompassing reality. So touch with Love wherever you can. It is the alchemy of Creation. Miracles are only miracles because the power of love seems a new experience to humankind. However, love is incredibly all powerful, and miracles will become commonplace in the lives of people, as you yourselves can now witness in your daily life. In the miracles of the matching of circumstances to your intents, the miracles of synchronicity of events, the miracles of the exponential power of the recognition of common ground between people. Spread the miracle of your love and watch how quickly it takes root and moves like wildfire.

## Weaving Your Dream

So the future of humanity is unwritten. It is contained in the potential of your becoming all that you can be. It will be determined by what you consciously bring into your focussed intent. It can be anything you desire and will be fired by your commitment to explore your potential choices. To sift through what brings you the experience of the qualities within that lead to feelings of enjoyment, fun, and harmonious expansion. No one knows, not even the Masters of Wisdom, what form human life will take because it is up to the choices you make and you are entirely free to make what will bring you the highest you can imagine.

It is known, however, that because of the shift in the collective human consciousness, the future of humanity on earth is assured and as we make the transformation it will be in the direction of unity, love, peace, and harmony between all. How long it will take, how it will be expressed, and how easy or difficult it will be to make the full transformation, is entirely up to us all, and the combined creational power of our vision and intent.

Your responsibility in all this is to experiment and explore your dreams. Your dream of what you really want to be, the quality of experience you yearn to have in your life, and what works for you. You need to explore your own uncensored dream of Paradise, and begin to envision it as, not only a possibility but a truth in the making. You are weaving your dream in the ethers of thought and excitement which will become your experience in a now that is becoming. Do not underestimate the power of your dream weaving. There are hundreds of thousands of others in this world who are doing the same. They are weaving a similar Paradise of their inspired, loving intent, brought forward out of the depths of their being. The combined power of that intent makes it easier for the next person to weave their own dream. It then becomes woven into the blueprint of the global reality to become the New human expression of life with Gaia.

Therefore, in building your highest vision for the future that you desire to bring into manifestation, you are performing great service to all humanity. Explore and discover what really inspires you. To be inspired is to be lifted up in spirits and to be keyed into something, some quality that brings you greater hope, greater expectation of possibility, a clearer vision of what you really want. Look to the sentiments expressed by people you admire. What would be an ideal world for you in relationships with others, in natural surroundings? What intents do you have for all humanity, what do you wish for all? What is your vision for the best for you, for earth, humanity, and all kingdoms? Begin to retrieve your memory of what you have known in your distant past, your times and feelings of greatest joy, and the places of beauty and grandeur you have experienced. Bring them back into your conscious dreaming to help provide you with options in your dream weaving. Sitting down with a group of friends to share your highest visions of the future will be a joyful and inspiring experience. How about a group vision board, where you each bring words and pictures, cut out of magazines, that inspire your dream of your world becoming, and paste them in a collage as you share them?

Remember that the New Reality of quantum magic, conscious manifestation of infinite possibility, is yours to command. We are all in the process of really coming to terms with what we are and what we want. No one can sit on the fence waiting anymore. It is too painful and with the build up of your energy, your light quotient, it is impossible to remain in one place. Choosing a direction to move is obligatory so make your choices from the best that are available to you in this moment. Of course your vision will change as you change but this is the wonder of being all you can be, a delightful surprise.

## Putting it All Together

If you have read this far there will be a good part of the journey we have made together that has touched you in some way. There will be parts that have resonated for you. No matter whether you have been on your journey for a long time or are just beginning to wake up to the enormity of what is happening to you, the only place to move on to is to that which fires your imagination, which speaks a strong "Yes" to you. There is no right or wrong starting place. There can only be Your Way for you.

The important thing is to do something different in your daily life if you want to experience something different. To build new daily practices that will support your new way of seeing and knowing. Therefore, the suggestions that follow are only guidelines, an example of what is likely to be helpful in developing a daily dynamic that will enhance the energy shift in you. A set of easy practices that will be based on your desire to be more of who you really are.

*********************

## A DAILY REMINDER FOR AWAKENING

To kick start your mindful awareness of taking increased charge of your life use the mantra "I Remember". Say it out loud to yourself three times when you are alone, and to yourself in thought when in earshot. Say it with feeling and let your thoughts go to the vision of your Being, your Higher, expanded, all loving and all knowing Presence, Your Self. If you cannot feel it at the time just imagine, or think as if it is true. Just allow your mantra to initiate your connection, know that this has happened instantaneously, and be with that without any agenda except to be open to your Presence. Use this mantra whenever you think of it during the day and then go on with what is in front of you. Whenever you stop in your daily activities come back to your mantra before you move on in thought or action.

You may wish to then focus on your breath, feel gratitude, express your passion etc. but start with a reminder from yourself, a reminder to be as present and connected as you can be.

Everything else that you choose to do follows your remembering. The more you remember the more you are with the best that you can be in that now. And the feeling of your Presence will grow with your conscious reminders. So remembering is key, and to help you remember other routines you choose to adopt I have found that to have a Code for Living your day is a useful and fun device.

## Code for Daily Living

The device involves listing up to ten intents, attitudes or things you will do for that day that you have chosen for yourself and that align you with the kind of person you are deciding to be. What activities can you most profit from in your daily life?

Your list will be your Code for Living this next day. You may not even fulfil them on that day but you will start your day with them in mind and incorporate as much of what you set yourself for that day. They will become your guidelines. And when you fall short you will not judge yourself, but you will note that experience, and accept what is, and take your Code on with you the next day.

Use a small card that you can keep in your top pocket or purse. Head it 'Living Code for Today' or 'My Ten Commandments'. Initially if 10 are too many start with three only, and then build up to ten. Feel free to change or modify any of these at any time. It can be altered daily, weekly, monthly or whenever you wish.

Do not admonish yourself if you do not complete or fall short of your intents for that day. Just continue with your code for at least a week then decide whether you drop any particular items for this time. What you set yourself should be enjoyable, inspiring, challenging but manageable. What you can accomplish today you may find unchallenging tomorrow, or something else may arise that is more relevant for that time. It is a matter of learning and practice. Practice in becoming more aware and more in charge of what you do, learning and experiencing about the emerging you. Old habits of thinking, feeling and doing are most easily seen, and fall away, when they are lovingly replaced by new ones.

I have provided an example list of often used Codes. These are not a set of 'shoulds', 'musts' and rules applied by some external authority. The codes you choose are reminders that are there to help you remember the person you are choosing to be, therefore your own Codes can be anything you wish. You will come up with others as you move into the practice. Your daily dynamic will change as your awareness and the needs of your journey make themselves known to you.

## Example:

### Living Code for Today

1. Just for today I will remember my highest expression as often as I can by stopping in my thoughts and saying "I remember" three times with a sense of my Presence.

2. Just for today, whenever I think of it, I will give thanks for what I have in that moment.

3. Just for today I will start the day with a request to my support family for the most benevolent outcomes for myself and all I come in contact with.

4. Just for today I will make a point of communicating with at least three others with a loving smile, touch, or word of kindness.

5. Just for today I will do something that I enjoy or can bring joy to, just for the sake of doing it and without any other justification.

6. Just for today I will listen to others or the media without any judgement or fear.

7. Just for today I will release in love and understanding, something in my past memory that has been difficult to resolve.

8. Just for today I will spend at least 10 minutes relaxed and gently watching my breath.

9. Just for today I will talk to my body and cells in a loving and encouraging manner.

10. Just for today I will read or listen to something that uplifts me.

The possibilities are endless. Sometimes I like to set myself a little fun mission. For example, I love this one, "Just for today I will do something for someone that they will appreciate, without them knowing. If they find out that it was me who did it then it will not count".

It would be better not to use the Living Code for Today technique if it becomes a chore. It is a device to act as an inspiring reminder of life choices you are making in amongst the noise and pressure of your day.

*********************

## Weaving the Web of Light and Love

Your energy field contains a beautiful web of light strands and filaments that hold the experiences and potential of all that you have been and are, and all the potential possibilities that you can create. It is instantaneously and eternally connected to All That Is. What you do, what you think, what you feel, is available to all. In the same way Gaia has woven her own web of all that she is and we are connected to her through chains of Love like golden necklaces that are vibrant and alive. It is what I call 'The World Wide Web of Light and Love'. Every time you have a feeling of Love and you have nowhere special to send it, intend that it go to this WWW. Ask your angels to take your Love to where it is most needed or to where it will do the highest good. Do not underestimate your power. As a human angel your energy has a special power to effect anyone, any creature, any mineral, any place or space on Earth. It is what you have come to do. To make a difference.

All it takes is a second of your loving intent to add to this great reservoir of creative outpouring. The WWW is growing and glowing with the input of hundreds of thousands of waking angels, remembering why they have come, and what they can do best. We can contain our love no longer and the more we tune into our joy the more boundless our love experience becomes. So join with us all as we create the New Reality through the discovery and sharing of what it is like to truly be alive.

## Your Acts of Love

Let us review, before the completion of this journey, how far you have come and how deep your love is.

1. Every moment you are here taking into yourself the energy of the Shift, is an Act of Love.

2. Every step you take to understand and embrace the New Reality, is an Act of Love.

3. Every step you have made to take the long journey and come into this incarnation at this time, is an Act of Love.

4. Every experience you have had to bring you to this point of transformation now, is an Act of Love.

5. Every thought and feeling of separation and unlovedness you become aware of and let go, with understanding and forgiveness is an Act of Love.

6. Every breath you take and sense in moving in and out of you as you watch, is an Act of Love.

7. Every time you take a moment to be present with yourself and your world, is an Act of Love.

8. Every time you see an event in your life that the Universe has brought to you and you say 'yes' to it, is an Act of Love

9. Every time you listen to the sounds, the song, the promptings of your heart and respond to it, is an Act of Love.

10. Every time you sense the Holy Presence and realise it is you, is an Act of Love.

11. Every time you consciously share your Light with the cells of your body is an Act of Love.

12. Every time you become aware of your energy bodies and energy field and consciously breathe in the Light, the breath it out to the world, it is an Act of Love.

13. Every time you consciously connect to the light centre of Earth and ground yourself, is an Act of Love.

14. Every time you connect to your support team and ask for their guidance and help, is an Act of Love.

15. Every time you sit to meditate and take the time to surrender to your Divine nature, is an Act of Love.

16. Every time you sense and feel your Oneness with anything in your awareness, is an Act of Love.

17. Every time you choose to follow your passion and do the things you enjoy doing, is an Act of Love.

18. Every time you express your gratitude for what is in your life, is an Act of Love.

19. Every time you direct your intent to something that you deeply desire, is an Act of Love.

20. And every time you look into the eyes of someone else and smile, or share laughter, or put out your hand and touch in friendship, or offer a kind word of encouragement, is an Act of Love.

And you say it is so difficult to love yourself. Think again my beloved human.

We are breaking through the conditioning of the past ages written in our DNA. When the rule of life becomes one of love instead of fear then we will be free. The quest for love, for power and direction has been outside of self. When you rewrite your doing always in terms of your internal Being then you will be living as an Enlightened One.

Of course it is easier said than done, but it is not too far away. To stand back, to watch and sense then to embrace and act, is what it is all about. By the simple acts of trust in your own process, your knowledge and competence, the truth of who and what you are must follow. It is the Law of your own Unfolding and must be so. Your life will be a full, joyous, and an ever expanding adventure of possibilities far beyond your present comprehension. You can build and intend your greatest vision of the world you dream of, but you cannot know the full glory of where you are going until you get there. Anyway, why would you want to know. It would spoil the surprise. A growing trust in yourself, by developing a memory filled with the experiences of the joy in taking your own power and direction, will carry you into a future of untold opportunities and miraculous outcomes.

CPSIA information can be obtained at www.ICGtesting.com
Printed in the USA
LVOW101913291111

257010LV00001B/276/P

9 780741 452855